MY HAWAII
1938-1962

MY HAWAII
1938-1962

With Personal Recollections of
Pearl Harbor
December 7, 1941

Jane Thomas

On the cover—From *War and Peace*

To order additional copies of this book, contact:
Xlibris Corporation
1-888-795-4274
www.Xlibris.com
Orders@Xlibris.com
17220

CONTENTS

To my family.

FOREWORD

Each generation remembers the good old days and the way things were. When I came to Honolulu in 1938, the Aloha Tower was the highest building in the city. Fort Street had the impressive office buildings of the Sugar Factors (the "Big Five" companies who each managed several plantations on the different islands), the fine stores of McInerny's and Liberty House below King Street, and Wichman's Jewelers and Watumull's import store above King Street.

Green growth was just beginning to creep up on the slopes of Diamond Head. The mahogany trees along Kalakaua Avenue were small. Kau Kau Korner was just past the Ala Wai Bridge on the Waikiki side, with its sign pointing every which way to give the distances to cities around the world. Farther along on Kalakaua Avenue was Lau Yee Chai's restaurant (Lousy's), a favorite place for dinner and dancing until the owner lost it in a gambling game.

Members of the Honolulu Outdoor Circle, organized in 1911, kept a presence at the meetings of the legislature until they managed to get a bill passed to make billboards illegal anywhere in the state. This has added greatly to preserving the beauty of the Islands.

There were three tourist hotels in Waikiki—the small, elegant Halekulani, the Royal Hawaiian owned by the Matson Navigation Company and familiarly known as the "Pink Palace", and the grand old Moana with its Banyan Court where popular band leader Harry Owens played his Saturday morning concerts. In the area of Lewers Street and Beachwalk there were only many small cottages.

The way over the *Pali*, the mountainous road from Honolulu to the little town of Kailua on the other side of the island was by the narrow and very precipitous switchback road down the cliff. Kailua had the old Coconut Grove, a casual nightspot for dancing. Kane'ohe was just the naval base for the old PBY "flying boats". Haiku Valley and all that side of the coastal highway were entirely wild—and available for hiking and ti leaf sliding and picnics and swimming in the mountain streams. The road on around the island was punctuated by small sugar plantation towns. Hanauma Bay by Koko Head was breathtaking with its subtle shades of greens and blues, pristine—and deserted.

And that's the way it was.

•   •   •

At the urging of family members, the memoirs of my life in the Islands from 1938 to 1962 were finally begun at Copper Mountain, Colorado, on June 22, 1996. After coming home to Opelika, Alabama, I found my calendar diary for 1942, which proved very helpful. The year is now 2002, and details of this account have been written with assistance from three of my friends who also remember that fearful day at The Queen's Hospital, the "Day of Infamy," when the Japanese bombed Pearl Harbor. To each of these three: Betty Carpelan McKenzie of Santa Cruz, California, Helen Nieman MacBride of Honolulu, and Helen Carter Weiss of Kailua, Hawaii, I give many thanks, with very special thanks to Helen Weiss who remembered important things that I had forgotten. Also special thanks to Cletis Brown of Opelika, Alabama, who kept encouraging me and typed my first effort at this account.

When my niece, Diana Etheridge, of Merritt Island, Florida, and Copper Mountain, Colorado, sent me her old laptop computer I began to write this story in earnest. With my son, Dr. James Thomas for proofreading and computer assistance, and Diana to edit and make helpful suggestions, writing it has been a labor of love. For their faithful help and constant encouragement I offer much gratitude.

THE WAY IT WAS
THE PRE-WAR YEARS
1938-1941

A life in the Hawaiian Islands in those blissful days was not even in the imagination of a girl who had grown up in Highland, Kansas. My travels (after we came down from Alaska when I was four years old) had been to the orthodontist in St. Joseph, Missouri, to Kansas city to the Nelson Art Gallery, to the Ozarks for a summer holiday and on more or less annual pilgrimages to Pennsylvania to visit my mother's family in West Alexander and Washington, and my father's family in Grove City and Pittsburgh.

And here I was on March 3, 1938, young and free in the Paradise of the Pacific. At the time I presumed the superiority of the haole (Caucasians), but I was fascinated by all the mixture of races here, and tried to figure out distinguishing features of the Hawaiians, Japanese, Chinese, Korean, Portuguese and Filipinos. I had learned that the first Europeans here were Spanish explorers looking for gold such as they had found in Mexico. Finding no metal at all in these volcanic rocks, they did not stay. Some two centuries later, in 1778, the Englishman, Captain Cook

rediscovered the Islands. Whaling ships then found this a
convenient stopover for replenishing food and water. Some sailors
jumped ship here and stayed. They found a well-organized social
structure under the reign of the great King Kamehameha. During
the nineteenth century the English, French and American
governments struggled for control of the Islands. Finally, in 1893
the reigning, sovereign Queen Lili'uokalani was forcibly deposed
and Hawaii became a republic. Hawaii was annexed as a territory
of the United States in 1898. The haole, some of whom were
descendants of the first missionaries from New England, then
acquired the best of the land and brought the other peoples as
laborers in their sugar and pineapple fields.

However in this world did I get to Hawaii? To begin with, I
had connections. My father, the Rev. John Lynn Howe, was
president of Highland College, a small junior college in the very
northeast corner of Kansas. The college was, by his design, really
a precursor of today's community colleges. He was well respected
for his work by Dr. Paul B. Lawson, the dean of Kansas
University. Therefore, when I graduated from Highland College
I went to the university as a junior. My father introduced me to
the dean, and I had the privilege of his guidance from time to
time.

At the university I decided on a major in bacteriology. The
Kansas department was rated tops in the country, with a very
superior faculty. The department head was Dr. Noble P.
Sherwood, an eminent immunologist. Dr. E. Lee Treece in
bacteriology, Dr. Cora Downs in hematology and Dr. Mary
Larson in parasitology were all outstanding professors.

My days were so filled with time-consuming laboratory
courses that I had little time for anything else. And it was difficult
to find one or two-hour courses, for which I had the prerequisites.
Dean Lawson helped find courses that would fit into my
curriculum and give me the credits I needed for graduation. When
he insisted that I take a course in Medieval Culture from the
professor considered the best teacher in the university, I was
concerned that I lacked the background for the course. The dean

was right in his suggestion, and I sat enthralled and in awe of what I was missing because of all the time-consuming labs. A two-hour course in Advanced English Literature found me in a class of all English majors and graduate students, but it was also a great experience. I also filled in with two one-hour seminars, in child psychology and finger-painting!

It was the depths of the Great Depression, and I had no money. I was grateful to be given a job in the stockroom of the bacteriology department, handing out supplies to other students. The pay was fifty cents an hour. I walked to school—most students did—and ate lunch in the student union building. There were two menus I could afford—a bowl of chili or a tuna sandwich. Each cost ten cents. The chili was the best buy, since there was plenty of catsup and all the crackers one wanted. Very occasionally I would splurge on a jelly doughnut and a cup of coffee or a chocolate marshmallow root beer. No one had any money, as a matter of fact. On a date we would have one coke, and you cannot imagine how long one coke can last. For special occasions there might be a twenty-five cent movie, but probably not a coke too.

At some time during my senior year but before I had taken Dr. Sherwood's course in immunology, he invited me into his private research laboratory. He had me watch while he performed a titration of "complement". This procedure involves the accurate pipetting of reagents into a row of test tubes in a rack. All pipetting was done by mouth using calibrated glass pipettes. When he finished, he moved over and said, "Now you do it." And I did! From then on I did his routine basic research in immunology.

Dr. Downs also asked me to assist her with some research. At that time she was the only laboratory specialist working with tularemia who had not contracted the disease. Tularemia (rabbit fever) is a bacterial infection causing high fever, recurrent chills and extreme weakness. Blood counts were done on infected rabbits at the height of fever, and I did not like even going into the room with the rabbit cages. It was necessary to fill a tiny blood counting pipette accurately with blood from the ear of an infected rabbit which was shaking with fever. My hands were shaking as I pricked the ear of the shaking rabbit. Somehow I got my shaking synchronized with the rabbit's shaking and got the blood counts done without becoming infected with Francisella tularensis.

Having lost credits in transferring from Highland College to K.U., and because of my work schedule and all those labs, I had to take a biochemistry course in the summer. I finished in January of 1938 and graduated with a major in bacteriology and a minor in chemistry. The next thing on my proper schedule should have been to go to Kansas City for a nine-month internship. Since my professors knew that I did not have the resources to support myself in the city and because of my experience, working directly with them, they were willing to give me a job recommendation without the internship. Trained technicians were in demand, and I had four job offers. I chose to accept a position with a private laboratory in Emporia, Kansas. This was a very practical choice because my aunt, Mary L. Chaney, taught in Emporia College, and I could live with my favorite aunt and her semi-invalid sister, my Aunt Edna.

In the mean time, Dr. Downs had once asked me if I had ever thought of going to the Queen's Hospital in Honolulu. I had not. The Queen's hospital was well known to K.U. since Clara Nigg, a graduate of K.U., had gone to work at Queen's in 1922. She was so good that, any time a new technician was needed, any applicant from K.U. topped the list. So, when Dr. Downs brought this up, I, of course, thought it a fine idea and sent an application. Even though it seemed a very unlikely thing, when I accepted the job in Emporia I stipulated that if an offer came from Queen's I would take it. After I had worked in Emporia one week I had a cable from Honolulu. I was offered a job at $75 a month plus room and board. I left quickly for home in Lawrence and got ready to leave for Paradise.

Passage was booked on the "Matsonia", one of four passenger ships of the Matson Line, and I boarded in Los Angeles. It was a four and a half day trip, and I loved every minute of it. I had had almost no time to play bridge in college, so was quite inexperienced, but was talked into joining a foursome. As luck would have it, I won all the way. I was traveling cabin class, of course, and there was no admission to first class, where the music and dancing were going on. To my delight the cabin stewards unlocked the doors every night for me and another girl so that we could go dancing in the first class section of the ship, with the admonition that we must be back before midnight, when they would secure the doors for the night. So, like two Cinderellas we made sure to be back on time. I have no recollection of the difference in the elegance of the first class section compared with cabin class, except that they had a dance band and we didn't. I remember only that we had a wonderful time.

The approach to windward Oahu was quite a surprise. There were sheer cliffs that appeared from a distance to be bare. Not a palm tree in sight. A diary that I kept for six weeks or so reads:

3/3/38   The mountains of Hawaii look like corrugated cardboard when you first see them.

Diamond Head juts out into the water.

No wonder people love it here. Aloha Tower welcomes you.

I threw all my pennies into the water for the diving boys.

Arah (Weidman), Olga (Budin) and Dottie (Gattman) met me.

Those lovely, lovely leis!

Beautiful hospital in a grove of royal palms.

Up the Pali and a beautiful, still day. A sight unequaled.

Over to Lanikai in the afternoon with Arah and Helmuth (Nieman).

To Kewalo for dinner at night and my first glimpse of Waikiki.

3/4/38   My first day as technician at The Queen's Hospital, Honolulu, T.H.

3/5/38   First trip to Waikiki Beach. I love the blue pottery on the "rose-beige towers of the Royal Hawaiian."

You don't have to swim in the ocean. You just lie down and play in the water.

In a letter written home I describe the beach this way: "The beach itself isn't a very large place. The Royal Hawaiian and Moana Hotels are side by side on the beach and that's all. There was also an Outrigger Canoe Club and another club with a beach house—and the ocean. Ah! The ocean. The water is a clear, delicate blue-green, my favorite shade. I still don't believe it for sure. What makes it such a color? You can believe almost any of the freak tales people will tell you—like rain out of a blue sky, or rain in one block and sunshine in the next. I couldn't believe those things either if the rain didn't get me all wet. They call it liquid sunshine here." Since there had been an ice storm in Lawrence at the time I left Kansas, I note: I am now used to the greenness, but I still gasp at the brilliant flowering trees, even though very few are blooming now in comparison with May. The exquisite night-blooming cereus you have always heard about blooms on a plant belonging to the cactus family. I was so surprised at that. Many of the trees and plants are imported, as the banyan from India."

3/7/38   Lab picnic at Lanikai. I ate fresh coconut and didn't like it. I love the sand on my feet and the sound of the surf.

And later:

3/12/38   Went down to see Arah off for the mainland today. Gosh, that ship was so white it made your eyes water—especially when the band played Aloha Oe. The diving boys stay on the boat until it turns around in the harbor, then dive from the first and second decks (to recover the coins as they spiral down into the water and swim back to the ship. As time went on I found that seeing a boat off always made the eyes water.)

3/13/38   So! This is Hawaii. Out to Kaneʻohe to Dr. Larsen's cottage. Only 16 miles from Honolulu, and you could be positive that you were a hundred miles from nowhere, and that a haole was practically trespassing on sacred Hawaiian soil. The backyard is a bamboo grove. Samoan orchids grow in the hills. Went hiking through bamboo, hau trees, an old rubber plantation with huge mango trees. Saw an ancient Hawaiian village, with execution block, plots that were for taro and rice. Went up the hill for a ti leaf slide. Most glorious time, but, Oh! those candid cameras! Back for a dip in an ice-cold mountain stream. Best swim I ever had.

So, life was very full and exciting from the first day.

3/19/38   Tea dancing (an afternoon dancing party) at the Young Hotel. Red carnation lei.

3/20/38   Church this morning at the Hawaiian church. Songs and sermon in Hawaiian. Drove out to Pearl Harbor and then to Olga's for tennis, dinner and bridge. Home early.

On my birthday on March 27th I received my first gardenia lei and a copy of Don Blanding's "Vagabond House", a collection of his poetry.

On 4/13 I had my first hula lesson from lovely Moana.

Social life was a whirlwind from the start until my body finally said "slow down". Copying from the diary tells the story best:

4/8   Watched the fleet come in this morning. A thrilling sight to see all those ships come into view.

4/9   The fleet is in! Good thing all 35,000 sailors are not loose at one time. The town would be deluged.

4/10   Church with Paul. Lunch in Waikiki. Looked through Ala Moana Park. Went out to the blow hole, where the waves force a fountain of water through a hole in the rocks. Dinner at Lau Yee Chai's.

4/11   Tea dance at the Young Hotel. Sukiyaki dinner at Ishii Gardens.

4/12   Dinner at Kewalo with Ensign Clifford Messenheimer.

4/13   Paul called tonight. Went down to the waterfront to watch a boat go out. Went up to Wilhelmina Heights to look down on the city and the harbor.

4/16   Dinner on the battleship Maryland with Pete Trepani. Drove to Hancock Landing. All the gobs were going "home". The streets swarmed with them. The Maryland was about a five minute ride out on a small boat. Nearest the landing was the flagship of the fleet— the U.S.S. Pennsylvania, decorated with flags for a party. (I later went to an afternoon party on the Pennsylvania.) There seem to be several kinds of ships in the navy- airplane carriers, battleships, cruisers, destroyers, tenders. The Maryland carries three planes, two 16 inch guns and thousands of tons of armor plate. Saw the books of rules and regulations for routines under various conditions. Every day special rules for the day are sent out. The navy must run perfectly!

4/17   Up at 4:45 for the sunrise Easter service in Punchbowl Crater overlooking Honolulu harbor. Honolulu is most beautiful in the twilight of dawn. Before we could see the sun rise over the mountain, its rays struck first the carrier Saratoga in the grey mist of the harbor, making it shine brilliantly white. The Lexington was next and finally the Ranger. The three carriers were anchored in Honolulu Harbor. These carriers have about 2000 men apiece and carry more than 150 planes each. They are regular little cities in themselves. They don't look as if they were built for pleasure or beauty, either, though it is a beautiful sight to see them steaming in to the harbor. The rest of the fleet is in Pearl Harbor.

After the service, to breakfast at The Tavern in Waikiki, picked up a lunch, and off for my first trip around the island. First to Pearl City—what a let-down—no city at all. Pearl Harbor is all of it, I guess. Climbed up Pupukea. Most beautiful. The bay below looked to be painted. Lunch on the needles under ironwood trees. Down to the beach to watch the waves and see the roaring caves. On around, eventually to Lai'e and the Mormon Temple. Home tired.

4/19   Date with Pete tonight. Wore my blue and white formal. We started out at Kewalo. Decided to go to Waialae to dine and dance. Nice place. And who should be there but Mr. and Mrs. George Vanderbilt, Jr., and Gloria Baker. Nice looking couple.

4/20   The fleet sails away tonight. Date with Pete. Back to Kewalo. Almost too tired to dance. Aloha! You are lucky if you make it back to the ship.

4/22   I get a kick out of the real waterfront at night. Down on River Street there are the big dark buildings of the piers on one side and the little wide-open waterfront cafes on the other side. On farther down is a government pier. When a navy ship is in it anchors at this pier. Japanese get concessions for funny little fruit stands, lighted by old yellow lanterns, where they sell pineapples, coconuts, bananas, papayas to the sailors. A little farther on are the docks where the Japanese fishing sampans come in.

4/23   To the Spring Festival at the Kamehameha Girl's School this afternoon. Beautiful million dollar grounds with everything in the way of equipment. Hawaiian food for more than 1100 people. Laulau, (which are pork, fish and taro leaves wrapped in ti leaves and cooked), with sweet potatoes and poi. Ate the poi with one finger, and it was good with the laulau. Never thought I would like it. The Hawaiian women wear holoku. Fat women are favored.

4/27   Nicki wants me to take a blind date tonight with an aviator, name of Wendy Gettel. Never did trust blind dates, but this one was a success. Nice person. Good dancer.

Had a sukiyaki dinner at a Japanese tea house, Ishii Gardens. Shoes were removed outside, and kimono and slippers provided. The slippers were worn only until we reached the room with the woven mats on the floor. The food was cooked in a charcoal broiler by a pretty, kimono-clad Japanese girl, while we watched. The tea house garden had a little shrine up on a knoll. In it was a picture of a Buddha with an offering of food and candles and incense to burn.

On April 30th, Don Mitchell, a teacher in the Kamehameha Schools, invited me to the annual lu'au of the Hawaiian Club of the Kamehameha Boys' School. They held it at their cottages on the beach. Specialty foods had been sent from each of the other islands by the boys' families. A pig was stuffed with red hot coals and buried in the imu (pit) early in the afternoon, with bananas and sweet potatoes. For three days preparations had been in full swing. All afternoon the boys and girls worked. Some made leis, some cut pineapple and others arranged the tables. At five the pig was taken out of the imu—all 125 pounds of him—and placed on a huge board amid the baked sweet potatoes and bananas. Mm, it did smell good. It was taken to the kitchen for carving.

The long tables were entirely covered with ti leaves and sprinkled with flowers. Specially cut leaves were placed for the plates. Our table (head table) was furnished with wooden dishes in the shape of leaves for the pig, coconut bowls for the poi and sea shells for the condiments. The only thing that was haole was the soda pop. The torches were lighted, a Hawaiian blessing was given and we took our places. The menu was as follows:

Menu

LUʻAU:			Hui Oiwi
Puaʻa kalua	roast pig		Oahu
Poi			"
Chicken luʻau	chicken with coconut milk and taro leaves	"
Lomi Salmon			"
Maia	banana		"
Uala	sweet potato		Molokai
Inamona	roast kukui nut		Oahu
Limu	sea weed		Kauai
Opihi	shell fish		Puna, Hawaii
Pahakai	red salt		Kauai
Alaea	red clay		"
Kokea	sugar cane		Waipiʻo, Oahu
Nioi	red pepper		"
Onion			
Haupia	white coconut pudding		Hawaii
Kulolo	brown taro-coconut pudding		
Aku	dried fish		
Halakahiki	pineapple		Molokai

The luʻau was served with the *kalua* pig in the wooden dishes, the poi in the coconut bowls, condiments in a shell, the lomi salmon in another shell, the squid on a tray. The pineapple was cored just inside the skin, and the fruit cut in long sticks. We just lifted off the top to take out a stick. There were pieces of sugar cane in a kou bowl on the table. Pieces of kulolo (a very rich pudding made of taro and coconut cream) were on pieces of *ti* leaf. After we finished eating we chewed on sticks of sugar cane. Then we sat on the lawn and watched as the girls sang and danced the hula to tell the stories and legends. Eventually the kids all went home and we had coffee and cookies and coconut candy and listened to some Hawaiian tales and legends. I added a maile lei and another gardenia lei to my collection. The *maile* lei, a very special lei made only of fragrant leaves, was *maile la nui* from the Panaewa forest on the island of Hawaii. Brought home a pineapple.

The Hawaiian Club, the "*Hui Oiwi*", means "club of the

native sons". Their motto is *Ua malama ia pono o Ka 'Aina e na 'opio.*—"The traditions of the race are preserved by the young people." (Note: Being invited to this special feast was one of the most memorable things that happened to me in these years.)

To continue a bit from the diary:

5/1/38   May Day. Worked today, Sunday: Schedule—11 blood counts, 30 urines, donors for four transfusions, spinal fluid for quantitative sugar cell count and differential smear. Rather a heavy day. To church tonight with Wendy.

5/2/38   May Day is lei day in Hawaii, but being on Sunday it was celebrated today. Went at noon to the city hall, Honolulu Hale, to see the lei from the different islands. The prize lei was a lovely blue thing of about a dozen strands of Chinese violets. The grand prize lei was always blue because the poet Don Blanding wills it so. Don Blanding inspired the celebration of Lei Day. Blue lei are quite rare here, and they are lovely. Perhaps blue isn't so common here because it really doesn't go with the coloring of the Hawaiians as it does with Caucasian coloring. Reds, pinks and yellows are for them. (A very popular song at the time went

> "May Day is Lei Day in Hawaii
> May Day is happy day out there
> All of the colors of the rainbow
> Millions of blossoms everywhere")

In the book "Vagabond's House" by Don Blanding there is a poem:

"Leis . . . for Remembrance"

> Will you remember when you go away
> The fragrance of ginger blossoms in a white lei?

Will you remember the blue of the sea
That melts into sapphire at Waikiki?
Will you remember how you used to wear
Pikoki like ivory wound in your hair?
Will you remember the moon in the trees;
The scent of gardenias borne on the breeze;
Sunsets from Tantalus, rainbows at sea;
Will you . . . I hope you will not . . . forget me?
Will you remember the shadowy beams
Of Vagabond's House in our city of dreams?
Will you remember the tropical nights
With native boys singing? The flickering lights
O fishermen prowling about on the reef?
Will you remember . . . the moment is brief . . .
When your ship sails away while your friends on
      the shore
Sing "Aloha, farewell, 'til we see you once more."

5/7/38   Sent Mother a Mother's Day cable. Dancing at the Young with Wendy. A three strand pikake lei. I love 'em.

5/8/38   Worked with Helen Nieman. Went home to supper with her.

5/10/38   With Wendy to the wrestling match starring the world champion, Mazurski, an ex-all American fullback, who utilized his tackle in wrestling. Didn't like.

5/11/38   Dancing at Kewalo with Wendy.

5/12/38   Hospital Day. Waxed eloquent concerning the technique and value of Wassermann tests to numerous lay audiences as I took charge of the laboratory display in the evening. Afterward to the Nurses' Home where the dietary department concluded the evening with ice cream, cake and coffee. Really had sort of a good time.

5/13/38   Friday the thirteenth and a total eclipse of the moon. Quite a striking sight to see a Hawaiian full moon in total eclipse!

     Next Friday I get to go with Don to the Kamehameha

Founder's Day ceremony at the only royal cemetery in America. Don says he knows the keeper, who will let us enter the mausoleum. There is only one puka (space) left for the last princess. When she dies it will all be sealed.

The diary fades away at this point, except for the words in Hawaiian of the songs that I liked best: *Ua Like no a Like, Ke kali nei au* (the Hawaiian wedding song), *Lili'u E* (a paen to Queen Lili'uokalani), The Piercing winds of Maui-Waikapu, Wailuku, Waiehu, Waihe'e—*Imi au ia 'oe, Kaimana Hila.*

When I arrived at Queen's, the Harkness Nurses' Home on the hospital grounds was fully occupied. The space available was in the Nurses' Annex, an old wooden structure with about twelve rooms. I put a stretched out map of the world on the wall, and each month when I banked my pittance I marked the distance I thought I might get toward the Orient. My absorption with science left me with little understanding of the wide, wide world, so I thought I would find out by experience. My intention was to work in Honolulu for a time, then get on a boat and head west, stop someplace that appealed to me and work there for a while before going on around the world. I used to go down to the piers with a friend and inspect ships from various countries to see how I would choose to travel. Swedish fruit ships took the prize for beautiful accommodations. As is the case now, some freighters took a few passengers. The general situation in the Orient prevented my completing these plans, however, and I spent the World War II years in the Islands.

As I wandered about, getting to know the city of Honolulu in 1938, I found Olga Yankoff's "Samovar" shop and was fascinated by the jewelry and other treasures from Russia. I was also fascinated by Olga Yankoff. One item that kept my attention was a belt of double silver links decorated with niello, which had probably belonged to an army officer in the Caucasus. The word "Caucasus" was inscribed on the buckle. I coveted that belt.

With my splendid salary of seventy-five dollars a month plus room and board, (later increased to ninety dollars), I was repaying my college loan and sending money home to my parents. And saving up for a vacation. I had to buy uniforms, shoes and other clothing, so the idea of a silver belt from Russia was quite absurd. However, I kept going back, getting to know Olga, admiring almost everything in the shop—and coveting that belt. Gradually I got to know Olga's story.

Olga Yankoff was the wife of a young Russian army officer. They had two small sons. The year was 1917. As she told it, one day soldiers of the Red Army came to their home in Moscow. She took her two sons and went out the back door practically as the soldiers were coming in her front door. Somehow she made her way all across Siberia to the city of Harbin in Manchuria. There she stayed for some years, not knowing the whereabouts of her husband. Finally she brought her boys to Honolulu and opened her shop of Russian imports. The older son became an architect. The other was a dancing teacher. Olga's knowledge of the Russian language made her in demand on state occasions so that she enjoyed some civic prominence.

Eventually it was arranged that I should go on Monday evenings to her home on the side of Punchbowl Crater to study the Russian language. This was destined to be quite an experience. Most prominent in the comfortably furnished living room was a very large silver samovar, which dominated the decor. Since there was no grammar book, I did not progress very far or very fast. I learned the alphabet and learned a song which we sang together soulfully, and she said my Russian name was Yevganya. Emotional Olga would talk about Russia with tears of happiness at remembering. After a while we would repair to the kitchen, where she had prepared some special food. This made her cry more happy tears. The things prepared were very good but quite different from anything I knew.

Then it happened.

It was about the fourth or fifth Monday evening, as I recall, when I was greeted by a very much-excited Olga. Her architect son had given her a new car!! She had never driven, so she said that since she had never accepted any remuneration from me for the Russian lessons I could repay her by teaching her to drive. The idea was terrifying. I had taught an aunt to drive when I was very young, but the personality was quite different, it was daytime and it was not in the middle of a busy city. In desperation I thought of a possible plan. We went down to 'Iolani Palace, which was deserted and had a circular drive around it.

There I put Olga at the controls and we started around and around, practicing shifting gears and braking. (No automatic transmission in those days.) Coordinating clutch and gear shift and clutch and brakes proved to be very difficult. When both of us were totally frustrated we drove back to her house. The next week the experience was the same, without any noticeable improvement. And Olga was getting impatient to get on with this driving business.

The next Monday I went again—with fear and trembling. Again I was met by a very much-excited Olga. The words tumbled all over themselves as she told me how she had decided to practice on her own, had managed to do rather well until the short return trip. Coming up a hill she came to a five-way stop. She was the lead car, and she had to make a left turn. She did stop, but when she thought she saw a way through, the motor stalled and her emotions took over. Managing to get started again, she went straight forward at some speed—straight forward into the traffic V and into the little grocery store that was directly in front of her. Waving her arms, she described how she went right to the back of the store, with bottles of pickles and olives crashing all around. So much for the new car.

I never did have the courage to go back to Olga's home. But, yes, at some point along the way I had purchased the silver and niello belt, which I wore with evening dresses in which I went dinner-dancing. And I cherished it.

By December of my first year in the Islands I was so well acclimated that I was wearing a sweater in the evenings and to work in the mornings, as were most other people. We thought it was winter. The only thing I remember about my first Christmas had to do with pennies. A co-worker and I had decided early in the year to save our pennies. At Christmastime we emptied our piggy banks and asked for the name of a family in need. With just our pennies we provided a full turkey dinner "with all the trimmings" for a family of four! That was painless charity.

I lived for a year or so in the Nurses' Annex before there was a room in the Harkness Nurses' Home. My room in Harkness was on the second floor with the surgical nurses. There was a swimming pool, and the dining room was next to the hospital. We each had a mailbox in the large lobby. It was very comfortable living. Social life continued according to our choosing. There was an occasional civilian date, but mostly we chose the Navy. After being at sea for a month they had plenty of money, which they didn't mind spending. Most dates were for dinner-dancing at the Young Hotel or the Royal Hawaiian Hotel or Lau Yee Chai's restaurant. We wore evening clothes—long dresses for us and tuxedos for the young officers, who always arrived with leis or corsages. My favorite dancing shoes were made of very soft gold mesh with flat heels—almost like dancing barefoot! The only time my date ever brought a corsage instead of a lei, was the only time I ever wore a strapless dress (borrowed from a friend in the next room)!

When the ships were at sea they were cruising all over the Pacific. As result I received French perfume, a lavalava (a printed cotton wrap-around skirt) from Tahiti, interesting shell lei from some other island, and a stuffed Koala bear from Australia from my friends when they returned. The bear's name was Oscar Sydney. Actually he came from Brisbane, but that did not seem an appropriate name for a bear. What endeared him to me most was that he had three plain black leather toes and one patent leather toe.

My friends on the cruiser Portland were crossing the equator for the first time, so they were "Pollywogs". Every ship that crossed the equator had a ceremony at which the Pollywogs were turned into Shellbacks. At the ceremony Neptunus Rex presided, with his Royal Scribe, Davy Jones, to make out the certificates of promotion. Neptune brought the entire court with him—Mrs.

Neptune, the Crown Princess, the Royal Baby, the Royal Barbers, the Royal Police and a sort of Gestapo peculiar to the Realm of the Deep, better known to all Pollywogs as the "All Wet Shirts", the royal Surgeon, the Court Jester, the Royal Navigator, the Chief Justice of the Royal Court, the Royal Devils and sundry other noblemen of the realm.

Before the ceremony a lot of rumors had been circulated concerning the ordeal, so that the imaginations of all the beachcombers, landlubbers, sea-lawyers, lounge lizards, parlor dunnigans, plow deserters, park-bench warmers, hitch-hikers, chicken-chasers, hay-tossers, chit-signers, four-flushers and liberty-hounds falsely masquerading as seamen had worked overtime on the nature of the initiation—especially the physical punishment—but it was actually very light. The costumes were all manufactured on board, and the characters who played the various parts made it lots of fun.

The certificate read: "Be it known to all sailors, wherever they may be, and to all mermaids, sea-serpents, whales, sharks, dolphins, skates, eels, suckers, crabs, lobsters, pollywogs, tadpoles and other living things of the sea, that Ensign C.C. Laster Jr., U.S.N., crossed the limits of the Royal Domain in latitude 00-00 and longitude 16-22 West, and has been found to be worthy to be numbered as one of our trusty Shellbacks."

Several of us dated officers from the same ships when they were in port and went to the same places to party. Whenever the U.S.S. Portland, a cruiser, was in port we dated three officers who were best friends from the same Annapolis class. My date was "Arky" Laster, who proposed to me at least once a month. I did not think that I was cut out to be a Navy wife. (Annapolis graduates are gentlemen by act of Congress, so they say. After living in Alabama, in the Deep South, I came to realize that Southern men were taught manners and courtesy from early childhood. "Yes, sir." "Yes, Ma'am.") These three friends were southern-born and delightful company.

One very happy day with Arky happened when the Portland had been in port for some time and our friends had spent nearly all of their money. It was a Sunday. Arky and I started out in the early afternoon with a poetry book in hand. We boarded a bus in downtown Honolulu. I believe that bus fare was ten or fifteen cents. We went first to Kaimuki and got off the bus for a chocolate malt. Using a transfer, we took another bus to the top of Wilhelmina Heights, where we got off, each sat on a rock and read poetry. It was a lovely afternoon. Eventually we got back on the bus and rode all the way to Kewalo Basin, arriving at sunset, to see Venus as a brilliant evening star. All this was on one bus fare. We then walked back to the Hospital—quite a long way!

Once we managed to talk our favorite dates into taking us to the Roseland dance hall after the hotel band stopped playing. This was a dime a dance place where folks dressed as we were didn't usually show up. We had our hands stamped at the door. The men were apprehensive, worrying about whether strange-looking men would try to dance with us. We had no trouble as it turned out. Perhaps it was we who looked strange!

Once when the U.S.S. Portland was in port, Arky took me to a Beaux Arts Ball with an Arabian Nights theme. We dressed in costumes. I made a simple harem costume with yellow shorts and sleeveless top of a cotton fabric and sheer purple pantaloons and veil and felt quite roguish. There were some wonderful costumes, especially the hats. One outstanding number was a "Carmen Miranda" design, an enormous hat covered with fruit and flowers. The evening ended with a very badly done strip tease. I had never seen one before, but it did not impress me. I thought it was supposed to be artistic!

Another good friend was stationed on a destroyer. When they were in port he sometimes invited me to dinner and a movie on board, if he happened to "have the duty". This was great fun. I would go out to Landing C, I think it was. He would send the captain's gig—a neat little boat with lace curtains—to the dock and I would ride in state to the ship. I don't suppose that I was actually piped aboard, but I felt as if I were. After dinner, the wardroom being quite small, the movie was shown on deck.

When the evening was cool, he would put his greatcoat around my shoulders.

It was always a pleasure to drive out past the fish ponds at Aina Haina and around Koko Head and Koko Crater just to look down on exquisite Hanauma Bay with its varieties of coral and unbelievable shades of blue and green in the clear water. A beautiful drive at night was on past Koko Head to the "Blow Hole". The mountains are quite rugged, and the sea crashes up against the black lava rocks. In the moonlight the white spray is fascinating. The Blow Hole is a hole in the lava rocks with a sort of cave underneath. When the waves come in they fill the cave and send the spray shooting into the air.

A trip on the Pali Road was gorgeous at any time. The road leads up through tropical lushness from the city of Honolulu to a pass between two mountains. I have seen the *Pali* (the precipice over which King Kamehameha I pushed the armies of Oʻahu when he unified the all the Islands) when the wind was so strong that I could scarcely stand against it. I have seen it perfectly calm, rainy, cloudy or sunny, and it was always a thrill to be there. On the road up there are waterfalls on the side of the mountain where the wind is so strong that the water is blown back up and disappears in a mist.

One memorable occasion was an evening picnic at the "Queen's Bathtub", which was out past the Blow Hole. Facing south, I saw the Southern Cross for the first time. There it was, low in the southern sky! That night we decided to drive on around the Island. On past Makapuʻu, we went, past Waimanalo, past Lanikai to Kailua. There we probably stopped at the coconut grove for our first beer. All along the east side of the island, past Kaneʻohe Bay and Punaluʻu and Kahuku, past Sunset Beach and Waimea and finally to the east of the Waiʻanae range of mountains, through Schofield Barracks, past Pearl Harbor and finally back into Honolulu. It was a long night but a lovely trip.

Another well-remembered night beach picnic was at Kailua Beach. This was the first time I ever broke a bone—in my toe, just walking on the sand! I was in the car with my boss (the pathologist) and his wife, and he dropped his car keys in the sand. Fortunately there were two carloads of us. The other car was able to go back to Honolulu for another set of keys and disaster was averted.

Life was wonderful. In 1940 war was raging in Europe, but I wrote in a letter to my parents that I thought I was probably in the safest place I could possibly be.

I enjoyed my work thoroughly. In what would seem now quite a primitive laboratory, everything was hands on. Blood counts were done from very accurate little pipettes, one for white counts and one for red. They were hand shaken, and the count very carefully transferred to a glass counting chamber with a grid, put under a microscope and actually counted, one count for white cells and another for red cells The differential count was done from a stained smear on a glass slide. Every piece of equipment was carefully hand-washed. When blood was taken from a vein, a glass syringe was used with a needle which we had sharpened on a wet stone. Nothing was single-use throw away. The urine bottles were glass; all the test tubes for chemistry and serology were glass and had to be washed. The chemistries and serologies were pipetted by mouth. The petri plates for bacteriology were glass. We had orderlies to do the "dish washing", except for the blood counting instruments. We technicians did that.

Animals were used for laboratory testing. There was one sheep and many rabbits and guinea pigs. The rabbits were used for performing pregnancy tests. One of the rabbits was a beautiful, big, white fluffy Angora which we could never use for testing. Apparently everyone contributed to her name, since it grew to be Betsy Wu Ella Bora Bora Genevee Honey Bun. We sometimes had her brought to the lab to visit if we had a slow afternoon, and she became quite a pet.

I worked first in hematology—blood work—then in chemistry and serology (the testing of blood for disease). When I had weekend duty by myself I also got to do the bacteriology. Our working hours were 7:00 A.M. to 3:30 P.M. Dinner, which was actually quite good, was at 4:30 in the dining room next door, but by 9:00 o'clock we were usually hungry again and would go to the nearby "greasy spoon" for a hamburger and milk shake, or some such.

I took the required examination to become a Registered Medical Technologist. I even got to make vaccines of house dust or animal dander for Dr. Nils Paul Larsen, the medical director of the hospital, who was a pioneer in treating allergies. These vaccines were specific for the house or the animal belonging to the patient, and were used as injections for desensitization. On Saturday morning and Sunday morning one technician worked alone. That is how it happened that I was on duty on December 7th, the morning that Japan bombed Pearl Harbor.

Those were the days before there were blood banks. Transfusions were used only in emergencies when the patient's family was unable to provide a donor. The hospital had a very carefully selected list of professional donors we could call. These were policemen and firemen—big, healthy Hawaiians. When the danger of war seemed imminent one of the firemen taught us some jujitsu right there in the laboratory. This was of course a matter for general self-protection. Believe it or not, I learned how to throw a good sized man quite easily. The only technique that I remember is how to escape if someone has hold of both wrists. I wish that I could have kept up with it. It would be good to know. One of the policemen invited us to the police pistol range to learn to shoot. I had never handled a gun and never want to own one, but this seemed like another self-defense strategy so several of us went. I made a score of 91 out of a possible one hundred, with a .22 Colt automatic at twenty-five yards.

Once I noticed a permanent stamp on the hand of a patient. Upon inquiring about it, I was told that it was really a mark of inferiority put on an Okinawan who went to Japan. Okinawa belonged to Japan, and there were no apparent physical differences, so the reason must have been cultural. The inhabitants of the main islands of Japan apparently thought they were much more advanced culturally, so they made sure there was a visible distinguishing feature.

Weekends usually meant going to the beach at Waikiki. Two piece swim suits were in vogue at that time. We had them tailored by a Japanese seamstress on Kalakaua Avenue. We selected the style and the fabric from her selection, and she made them to fit. I preferred Grey's beach to the beach in front of the Royal Hawaiian Hotel. Grey's is a smaller beach between the Royal and Halekulani hotels. My aim was to get as much tan as possible without burning so I maintained a good tan. On some weekends there were invitations to someone's beach house on another part on the island.

After I had been there for a year it was time to plan a vacation. I enjoyed the company of Madeline Gentry, a beautiful red-headed nurse, the one who accompanied me to inspect the ships at the waterfront for future travel plans. We decided to go to one of the other islands and chose the island of Hawaii. We made reservations at the Kona Inn. Travel was by inter-island steamer. Ours was the S.S. Wai'ale'ale. We had heard about the Punahou School students traveling steerage. This meant that they were on the afterdeck with no staterooms. The ship left Honolulu at 4:00 in the afternoon and got into Hilo at 7:00 in the morning. The students spent much of the night with their guitars and ukuleles, singing and dancing hulas. The thought appealed to us, and besides it was cheap and would leave more money for other things. So we decided to go steerage, too. My friend, Madeline, and I had one problem. The kids traveled in jeans, but ladies did not. It occurred to us that there would be horses in Kona, and we could ride there. The solution was to wear our riding habits (jodhpur pants and boots), which we did. We often went horseback riding on the beach at Wai'alae.

However, the steerage idea did not appeal to my boss, the pathologist. He and his wife came down to see us off—with much apprehension. This increased when it became evident that there was an inebriated man on the afterdeck. It also became quite clear to us that he would be quickly taken care of if he made any inappropriate moves. So we set sail. The huge line that secured the ship in port was coiled at the stern, and we chose it for our spot. We could sit on it to watch the entertainment, and it was long enough for us to lie on. And sure enough, there were musical instruments. We settled down to enjoy the voyage. When dinner time came we found that there was one bit of information that we lacked. There was no way to get from steerage to the dining room. The gate between the steerage area and the rest of the ship was securely locked. Salt air makes a person especially hungry. We were hungry. The entertainment helped, and when it finally quieted down, we stretched out on our coil of rope to sleep. All we had for cover was our beach towels, so it was rather a chilly night, but apparently we did sleep. At about four o'clock in the morning we woke up—and there was Venus in the eastern sky—looking enormous and brilliant.

When we docked at seven, we went to the Hilo Hotel to wash our faces and have some breakfast. We rented a car and started on our very deliberate way toward Kona, stopping all along the way. The road was narrow and had almost no traffic. The day wore on toward evening and we were not yet at Kona; in fact it was dark when we arrived. We were met at the door by a much relieved hotel manager, George Cherry. He took us in to a very pleasant lounge with a big fireplace and brought us a drink—before telling us that the dining room was already closed. But, he said, taking a clue from our story, he had not yet eaten, and he usually ate steerage. This proved to mean that he ate by himself in what he referred to as his "crow's nest" from which he could view the dining room. And he had special food prepared. We enjoyed dinner each evening in the crow's nest.

As with all the islands, the scenery on the Big Island is spectacular, from desert to great lava flows to lush green canyons with lovely waterfalls and a coastline of black rocks or black sand and blue and white water. And four magnificent mountains— *Mauna Loa* and *Mauna Kea*, both nearly 14,000 feet tall, *Hualalai*, 8,000 ft., and *Kohala* 6,000 ft. As we continued on around the island, the most memorable stops were at Laupahoehoe Point, a spectacularly beautiful scenic point of black lava rocks at the foot of a cliff where the waves come rushing in to send mountains of spray into the air, and 'Akaka Falls, a 420 ft. waterfall in a lushly tropical setting.

The next year we took an apartment in Waikiki for a week, to have lots of beach time and also to pay our social debts by having company for dinner each night. This entertaining drained the money supply, so we thought we would try another steerage adventure to Kaua'i for the second week of our vacation. A cosmetologist friend told me of a Japanese hotel in the port town of Nawilili where she would stay for a dollar a night. That was about right for us. So off we went on another overnight trip. Upon arrival we went to the little hotel to register and get some breakfast. The hotel proprietors were not at all sure about this blonde and redhead. It must have been our traveling costumes, the jodhpurs and boots which confused them. Being very careful of the reputation of their hotel, they consulted for some time before declining to give this blonde and redhead a room—or even breakfast. They had brought us a glass of orange juice while they deliberated. But they were not taking any chances.

Another dilemma. The only other hotel was in the town of Lihue, a couple of miles inland. We started walking, with our suitcases and our grass beach mats. At the Lihue Hotel we were greeted by the proprietor-owner, Mr. Harold Rice. He provided us with a room in a little cottage. The furnishings were an old iron bed, a chair, one light—a bulb on a cord long enough to reach to the head of the bed, and a bathroom with a proper tub on legs. Mr. Rice said that his brother, state Senator Charlie Rice was in Honolulu, and we should use the beach at his home in Nawilili while we were there.

We went into town to the store to get sweet rolls for breakfast and meat and buns for lunch. Carrying our mats, we walked back to Nawilili the next day to Charlie's beach, which was very nice. That night we went to see a movie of some sort in the hotel lobby. Two salesmen were there who offered to take us with them the next day, when they would be going past Waimea Canyon, Hawaii's "Little Grand Canyon". We ordered box lunches for the next day. The lunches were very generous, and we had a great day. One day Mr. Rice said he had to go to Haena, which is at the remote end of the island, with marvelous scenery all the way. He very thoughtfully provided the lunches. When it came time for us to check out, he gave us our bills—$7.50 each. That was for four nights and a box lunch. He undoubtedly noticed that we did not show up in the dining room for meals, and that we walked everywhere, and realized that we did not have much money. The trip home was on, the *S.S. Humu'ulu*, which proved to be a cattle ship—complete with cattle in the steerage area. We had to spend down to our last dollar to rent mattresses for "deck space" and sleep on the deck. In fact, we had just enough money left to get home from the dock in Honolulu.

Periodically, Madeline and I made arrangements to visit ships that were docked in the harbor, to compare accommodations. There was a great deal of difference between the ships of different nationalities. Some freighters offered a few cabins for passengers. The Swedish fruit ships were the best. The cabins were well-appointed staterooms, and the ships were beautifully clean. Once we were given permission to visit a Japanese ship, the *Asama Maru*. When we went aboard we found that we were not at all welcome. Perhaps they had accommodations for Japanese tourists, but they had no interest in our traveling with them and did not show us any rooms.

Another short adventure Madeline and I had was a week-end trip to Moloka'i on a small vessel. The Moloka'i Channel is rough, so we took along a leafy branch. Just in case. (The sure cure for seasickness is to sit under a tree.) We left Kewalo Basin at three o'clock Saturday morning and trolled for fish on the way, sitting on the afterdeck with a jug of wine. I got very sleepy and tried to sleep on a seat in the cabin, holding on to the arms since it was quite rough. If I fell asleep I also fell off the seat so I gave that up. Fortunately we did catch a large mahimahi. I say fortunately because that is what the captain seemed to be counting on as the main food for the trip. As I recall, Madeline and I were the only passengers, so it would have been easy enough for the boat owner to shop for food at a market in the little port town of Kaunakakai if he needed to do that.

At the pier at Kaunakakai we were met by the mayor's son, with his guitar. He offered to show us around. We had gone to the Health Department and had passes to go down to Kalaupapa, the small peninsula containing the leper colony. Of course, it being a week-end there was no one available to open the locked gate at the top of the 2000 ft. cliff which separated Kalaupapa from the rest of the island, and so we were not able to go. This was a disappointment, but the trip up to the top of the cliff was beautiful. Looking down the straight-up sheer cliff was quite spectacular. It was a beautiful little peninsula, easily approachable only from the sea because of the sheer cliff wall. There were buildings and a little church which had been built by Father Damien, the priest who chose to go and live among the lepers, to care for them. We saw the town of Kaunakakai and a bit more of the island. We were intrigued by all the WANTED signs at the post office. This seemed such a remote place, but of course it would have been a fine place to hide. We were able to sleep better that night in the quiet water of the harbor rather than on the rough channel between Oʻahu and Molokaʻi. On Sunday we sailed back home.

My other deep-sea fishing trip was again into the Molokaʻi Channel, but was just a Saturday adventure. I have no idea what inspired me to go on this trip. I was just along for the ride. Sure enough, the sea was rough. There were a dozen or so of us on this trip. There was very little fishing done, as I recall. Almost all of them except Jane spent most of the time at the railing being ill, perhaps because no one thought to bring along a tree branch! When lunch time came the skipper produced what he had prepared for us. Guess what—avocado sandwiches—the same color as all the passengers. Those who had the courage to consider lunch took one look and went back to the railing.

I have never stopped being somewhat astonished at my varied Island experiences. As I have said, at The Queen's Hospital we used police and firemen as professional blood donors. (The Honolulu Blood Bank did not become active until the beginning of World War II.) One of the policemen took Nancy Leming and me "slumming" one night. He was in uniform. The first stop was a bar where the bouncer was a woman who bounced with a beer bottle. Even though we had a uniformed escort two men asked us to dance. The officer suggested that they go elsewhere. Next he took us for a quick walk-through to see how the different populations lived. Chinatown first. He took us then to an opium den where old Chinese men with wispy grey beards and queues in their hair sat in a large barn-like building smoking their water pipes. Philippine territory next, with its neat rows of small houses. Finally we went to the immaculate Japanese area which had well-tended window boxes of flowers.

Chinese were among the first immigrant sugar workers. Chinese families are close-knit and very industrious. They saved from their small wages until they could leave the plantation and open a small store close by. These appeared all over the Islands. Some of them moved into the towns and into Honolulu to open larger stores, bakeries and dry cleaning businesses. As they prospered, children were sent to the mainland for educating. One would go to medical school, and one to law school, being supported by the others at home. Thus the families became totally self-supporting and prosperous.

One remarkably unusual experience happened when my favorite among the hospital interns took me to visit the establishment of a famous "madam". She was famous both in Honolulu and in California, since she was a member of a very prominent West Coast family. We went rather late in the evening and had to be identified at the door before we were admitted. "The girls" were always in and out of the hospital, so the doctors became well known to them. We were taken into a very comfortably furnished lounge with only a few tables, rather more like a private club. The drinks were very weak and very expensive. There was no sign of the chief business. The madam must have paid dearly for police protection and probably lived in constant fear of the wrong police turning up and closing the place. Without any means of comparison, I would assume that most such houses were neither as elegant nor as discrete as this one.

As I have said, surprising things were always happening. A very handsome young Guamanian man came one day and offered to give rhumba and tango lessons. About a dozen of us signed up for the class, which was to be three rhumba and three tango lessons. The evening of the last tango lesson he asked me to dance with him. I was to close my eyes and hold up my right hand just to touch the fingers of his right hand and thus follow his lead. I couldn't imagine how this could work, but it felt wonderful. At the end of the dance there was enthusiastic applause from the interns' cottage next door. The side of their building was just window screen, as was that side of ours. I did go dancing with him a time or two after that, and he asked me to consider dancing with him professionally! We would have made a striking couple, with his black wavy hair and my long, sun bleached, blonde hair.

At that point in time, doctors were required to be a resident in the Islands for three years before they were licensed to practice. Therefore it was the young doctors just out of medical school who applied to intern at The Queen's Hospital. Since they were paid almost nothing at all they lived on the grounds in the "interns' cottage", which, in appearance, was quite comparable to the nurses' annex where I lived at first.

One of the interns at the hospital was the seventh son of a wealthy Spanish family in Nicaragua. He was tall and slender, with dark wavy hair and patrician features. All of his brothers had gone to "public" (private) school in England. He chose not to do this. He went to a public high school in Canada and to McGill University and medical school before coming to Queen's as an intern. In his spare time he frequented the little shops in Chinatown, looking for treasures. He did not live with the other interns, and one day he invited me to his apartment for tea and to see his latest treasure. We had tea, listened to beautiful music and admired his treasures. The latest was an exquisite white porcelain figurine of the Chinese goddess Quan Yin housed in her own beautifully lined wooden box. The figure was about ten inches tall. I believe he said that he paid fifty dollars for her, though she was probably worth hundreds. I showed him my wrist amulet of moss jade, which was the only purchase of much consequence I had made in these fascinating little stores.

The jade amulet was about three-fourths of an inch by two inches. It hung on a black silk cord with a tasseled end and a large carnelian drop. It separated to reveal a tiny carved Quan Yin inside. There were inscriptions on both sides. Later, one side was easily translated by a Chinese calligrapher in Honolulu. He thought the other side was written in ancient Korean, and I could not find anyone here in the Islands who could read it. Eventually I sent a rubbing to the Metropolitan Museum in New York. They replied that no one there could read it, and that the only person they knew of who might be able to read it had gone from the Metropolitan to the National Palace Museum in Taipei, Taiwan. So I sent a rubbing there. The reply follows:

"Thank you for your letter of 27 December, 1974. In examining the rubbing from the amulet, we have identified the inscription on the right side of the sheet as six Chinese characters, 'Ch'ien lung kuei-ch'ou nien tsao'. These six characters indicated that the object was made in the kuei-ch'ou year of the Chien-lung period. The year kuei-ch'ou represents the fifty-sixth year of Ch'ien-lung reign and is equivalent to the year A.D. 1793 in the western calendar.

The other portion of the rubbing is four Manchurian characters. The two characters on the right side should be read as 'gingguleme niyan' which means 'to offer respectfully'. The left two characters are difficult to recognize, but we assume that they might represent some person's name.

Sincerely,
Li Lin-ts'an
Deputy Director and Acting Curator
Department of Antiquities"

The answer from the Metropolitan Museum says, "As you may know, the Ch'ien-lung emperor was Manchu, and he frequently had things inscribed in both Chinese and Manchu . . . . May I add, by the way, that pencil rubbing was the best way to transcribe the engraved characters. Too often we receive well-intentioned but illegible characters hand copied which are of no help to us." Signed, Marilyn Fu, Assistant Curator, Dept. of Far Eastern Art.

The hospital interns were hired by and under the direction of Dr. Nils Paul Larsen, who also hired me. I revered Dr. Larsen, a man of boundless energy and bright blue eyes. A graduate of Cornell Medical School, he had come to the Islands in 1922. He founded The Medical Group, where I later worked. Group practice was a very new concept. Besides this private practice, he was Medical Director of The Queen's Hospital, the city hospital which had been founded by Queen Emma the wife of King Kamehameha IV, a tireless worker for the welfare of her people. Having charge of the interns and medical residents Dr. Larsen was able to keep the sugar and pineapple plantations supplied with doctors when they were needed. The plantations on the various islands had their own hospitals. When there was an opening, Dr. Larsen placed his doctors there. He then required monthly morbidity and mortality reports and published a monthly "*Plantation Bulletin*". Years later he received the Gold Cane award, which is the highest national award for industrial medicine.

Located in the middle of the Pacific Ocean, the Hawaiian Islands are a natural stopping place for anyone traveling from the mainland United States to Australia or the Orient. Dr. Larsen was well known all over the country, so famous doctors would stop to visit the hospital when they were traveling. Dr. Larsen had a regular Thursday morning clinic, when any special cases were reviewed and studied. He always asked the noted doctors to speak at these meetings. And he gave permission to any of the laboratory staff who were free at that he time to attend these meetings. This was a very special privilege.

Dr. Larsen was also an artist of note. He was a superb underwater photographer, painted with oils and water colors and learned etching and color etching from his neighbor, the well-known artist, John Kelly. A world traveler himself (he especially liked to ski in the Alps), Dr. Larsen took photographs of children's teeth all over the world, making a comparison of tooth health and diet. He was aware of the importance of vitamins and trace minerals many, many years before they were mentioned in popular literature. While on his world travels he was decorated by the king of Siam and the king of Sweden.

Following an illness, Dr. Larsen had severe angina and went to the mainland to be one of Dr. Paul Dudley White's first eight heart patients. I believe that his surgery was a vagotomy. He left on the Matson ship "Lurline" on December 5, 1941.

The letters I wrote home during these years indicate increasing concern for the escalation of threats of war in Europe. As was true of most Americans, I think, I was strongly against our involvement. I discussed my distrust of Mr. Chamberlain and my fear of Hitler. In April of 1941 Hitler was to make a speech scheduled for 12:30 A.M. our time, which I planned to stay up to hear. A new young intern brought a radio to the laboratory one day to listen to a speech by Hitler. He had had his training in Vienna, and I was shocked to see by the worshipful expression on his face in reaction to the speech that he had apparently been thoroughly brain-washed! In September of that year I came home from a party one night to find an "extra" under my door announcing the bombing of Warsaw. My comment was that I was almost afraid to go to sleep, realizing that war had begun in earnest. However, a letter of mine in August, 1940, stated that I thought there was no place in the world where I would be any safer than right here. I spoke of the variety of books I had been reading, including "Berlin Diary, a foreign correspondent's day-by-day account of Germany from 1934 to 1941". My comment, "It is amazing how clearly this foreign correspondent evaluated events at the time, and how right his reactions to the apathy of France and Britain have proved to be." Another letter reports on

Japan: "The Emperor, His Royal Highness, son of Heaven, seems a bit displeased by the unfriendly attitude displayed by the British in the unfortunate incidents they have figured in here in the Pacific." The incidents are not named.

Mail was sometimes very slow, depending on boat schedules. One letter of January 25, 1940, reports: "I finally got your long-delayed 'Clipper' letter (Pan American clipper, cost of a stamp, 20 cents) last week on the boat. We have been having bad weather between here and the coast, so that there has been only one Clipper since Christmas." Another letter says "The Matsonia is in dry dock, so no Matson mail this week. The other boats are going to Australia and the Orient." (cost of stamp, 3 cents). And, "Dear Mother, You can't guess. Today I received a letter from you mailed to me aboard the Lurline (the Matson liner on which I returned from the mainland). By the markings on it have figured that it has traveled approximately 14,000 miles—a round trip on the Matsonia and a round trip and a half on the Lurline. More than halfway around the world to get to me here." (In 1956 an airmail stamp cost 6 cents.)

In 1940 I was asked to help with the U.S.O. party plans for sailors. "We dressed ourselves up in our very best formals to go to the party", I said in a letter home. "The first party really was a picnic. These sweet boys would say things like, 'I'm kinda nervous. You are the first girl I have talked to in five months.' Nancy's and my favorites were a darling red-headed, freckled-faced kid and a very handsome marine. Only three or four commissioned officers were there as chaperones. We danced until we nearly collapsed, and I slept through breakfast this morning, although the party closed at 11:30."

A letter early in 1941 provided a bit more levity. "I stayed last night with a Navy wife whose husband has gone to sea. We had just showered and gone to our beds when we heard a noise outside which sounded like someone hitting a gong. It continued regularly, however, and the sound was more like an animal in the garbage can. We took flashlight in hand and looked in. It was a young rat. These varmints carry typhus fever so we had to kill it.

She impulsively threw a rock in, which only made a noise. Then we thought—drown him like a rat! We went to the kitchen and got a dishpan full of water and dumped it in. There sat the rat on the rock. Another pan full. Around and around went the rat in fine swimming form. The plumber's plunger holding the rat down contained plenty of air for him to breathe, as we decided after two attempts at holding him down this way. But the plunger on the rat with his nose sticking out proved readily effective. Next morning we had to dump out all that water and put the rat back into the can. One never knows what form of excitement will turn up next!"

A letter to my brother records: "Sometimes it gives one a rather undefinable feeling to look out at this Pacific Ocean. Right after dinner a couple of weeks ago, three of us climbed the face of old Punchbowl Crater to watch the sunset. From there we could see from Diamond Head on the one hand to Pearl Harbor on the other—and as far as we could see, there was the Pacific. At such times you take turns gloating over the beauty spread before you and hoping, hoping you will always be where you can see it, and being terribly conscious that this is a very small rock sticking up for some reason in the middle of a very, very large ocean. Then you almost want to hang on to something, and then quickly you marvel that there are cars and busses and even trains here and that each of them has been brought over two and a half thousand miles. Then a ship maneuvering out of the narrow little gate to Honolulu Harbor catches the light of the sun and sails away into the endless water in a blaze of light. For a moment then you feel at one with every boy who ever lived by the sea and waited to start living when he could sail away in a ship. As the sun goes down we start sliding back down the rocks to the city". (There is almost no twilight here. The sun disappears into the western sea, and darkness follows very quickly.)

An urgent letter was written to my father about some real identification for me. Since I was born in the territory of Alaska when it was very primitive and there were no social services, certificates were not issued or registered. So I was a non-person, and was uncomfortable with that situation with the imminence of war with Japan. Remarkably, the physician who attended my birth was available to write attesting to my legality. That paper is all I have in lieu of a birth certificate. There is something remarkable about this physician from Alaska being resident in Kansas City, Missouri, and my parents living ninety miles away in Lawrence, Kansas. Never mind that his records showed that I was a boy.

After being here for three years, I went back to Kansas to see my family in June of 1941. Things were getting rather tense in the Islands because of the threat of war with Japan—somewhere out there. Certainly, not here. However, realizing how absolutely dependent we were on ships and feeling that this was now my home, I took letters saying that I was indispensable in my job. Of course they would not mean much, but I had to do what I could. I was gone for a month but back well before that infamous day in December when the Japanese bombed Pearl Harbor.

THE DAY THE SKY FELL
DECEMBER 7, 1941

Sunday morning, December 7, 1941, was a day like any other perfect day in Hawaii with clear blue skies and a few puffy white clouds. It was a quiet weekend. The surgery at the Queen's Hospital in Honolulu was closed except for emergencies. The laboratory was staffed by one technician to take care of the necessary routine. I was that technician. And who would have believed that "HAWAII AT WAR!" would scream in the headline of the Honolulu Star-Bulletin later that day. I had gone on duty at seven o'clock as usual, along with Melba, my Japanese aide. I had taken care of the specimens that had come in since noon on Saturday, collected the blood counts that had been ordered, and was beginning to do the counting.

But my story must begin some months before, when I took a mainland trip in June of 1941 and took a letter from the hospital saying that I was indispensable. Happily, no emergency arose during the month I was away, and I returned to Honolulu to my lovely life of being young, blonde and single in beautiful Hawaii. As the months went by the tension grew. One day in the laboratory we found Hugo, our young Filipino orderly, examining a set of autopsy knives, carefully handling and balancing each one. Hugo told us that where he came from two brothers with bolo knives could stand off ten men. Somewhat later one of the knives was missing—and never showed up again.

On December 5, 1941, Dr. Nils Paul Larsen, Medical Director of the Queen's Hospital, and his wife left on the Matson ship Lurline to go to New York for heart surgery. He was one of Dr. Paul Dudley White's first patients. Also on that ship was our bacteriologist, Miss Nancy Leming, who went to visit her parents in Kansas City and did not return.

The young naval officers I dated came back from each month at sea with more and more apprehension. On November 30th I had a date with a lieutenant who had been out on a destroyer with a cruiser-carrier group somewhere in the Pacific. He was obviously quite tense when he made this comment—"We have got to be at war within a week!"

And so we were. Just before eight o'clock that Sunday morning, the earth began to shake. We were rather used to earthquakes, but this seemed different. The laboratory was on the fourth floor of the very open-air hospital (no air conditioning in those days). There was a rooftop library on this level, between the laboratory and the surgery. I went out on the rooftop to see what I could see.

Looking toward Pearl Harbor eight miles away I watched beautiful formations of planes circle and dive low over the harbor. This seemed very strange, since we had not heard of any maneuver exercises being planned for that weekend. There was also lots of smoke. I wondered if something had happened to ignite the huge fuel tanks on the hill. Strangely they were never hit.

The earth kept on shaking. I would do a blood count and then Melba and I would go out on the roof to look toward Pearl Harbor. What I saw was very puzzling. I would go back in and do another blood count or read out the bacteriology, then go back out on the roof.

The flight pattern of the Japanese planes was over Pearl Harbor. Not many flew directly over the city of Honolulu. The nearest bomb or shell explosion was a few blocks from the hospital. Four or five planes did fly so close to the hospital that I could see the pilots. They must have thought me out of my mind to be standing there on the roof watching them. The Japanese flag was not being featured in U. S. magazines at that time, and I was puzzled by that big red circle. Not Australia. Not Canada. The idea of a Japanese attack was completely inconceivable. The military might of our country was concentrated in Hawaii. We were surely protected on all sides! *Surely* we were.

It was not until the casualties began to arrive that we could begin to accept the truth of the situation. Even today, I can see Melba's face and the fear and uncertainty in her eyes when we finally realized what was happening. (As a matter of fact, I had no doubts about Melba's loyalty to the United States.) Inexplicably the electricity in the hospital failed, and there was no back-up generator. (Could this have been sabotage?) The surgery was on the fourth floor, so the patients had to be carried up on stretchers. Civilian casualties lined the front hall of the hospital, waiting their turns. It so happened that a Dr. Chang was performing an emergency appendectomy that morning with the assistance of a surgical nurse, Miss Betty Carpelan. After the attack, most of the civilian doctors went out to help at Tripler Army Hospital, the largest military hospital. The doctors who were at Queen's were Dr. Forrest Pinkerton, Dr. Ralph Cloward and Dr. C. M. Burgess. The resident physicians were Dr. Barton Eveleth and Dr. Ivar Larsen. They went out to Tripler, I believe. The interns at that time were Dr. Harold Sexton, Dr. Fred Warshauer, Dr. E. F. Slaten, Dr. Ted Casey, Dr. Robert Bailey and perhaps one other.

One of the doctors came back from working at Tripler Army Hospital to report that all of their extra emergency instruments were locked in a vault underground—not sterile and of course not ready for use. I was reminded of the day in September three months earlier when Ed, a sales representative for a pharmaceutical company, called at our laboratory.

Our laboratory was not one of his larger accounts. On this day, he sat talking with me and telling me of his concerns. He made regular visits to Tripler, the large Army Hospital, and was concerned with their lack of preparation for any great emergency. Ed said that Tripler had only one pound of sulfanilamide. Sulfanilamide, which came as a white powder, was the new wonder drug for treating wounds. Ed had gone back to Tripler several times, trying to convince them to stock more of the drug, but they failed to see the need. So, Ed told me, he ordered a great deal—many, many pounds on his own account. He would have had to pay for this if the need did not materialize. This was a very caring man, willing to take great personal responsibility for the welfare of the service men who were there to protect the rest of us.

How often I have thought of what a difference Ed's courage and foresight must have made to the men wounded at Pearl Harbor on December the 7th. The Navy was the buffer of defense for all of us. The Naval hospital on Oʻahu was not very large, since most medical needs were taken care of aboard ship. Tripler Hospital, on the other hand, took care of the large contingent of Army and Air Corps based on the island. Immediately after the attack on Pearl Harbor, Tripler had to supplement the field hospitals in caring for the casualties. Only civilian casualties were cared for in the city hospitals. Ed's decisive action surely saved an untold number of lives.

The Red Cross had just been starting a Blood Bank for Honolulu, and I believe there were about 230 units of plasma available. These were sent to Tripler and undoubtedly saved many lives. The hospital was still using policemen and firemen as professional donors, when families could not provide needed blood for transfusion. This small group of professional donors of various blood types was usually available. But not that day. Therefore I had quite a dilemma.

My supervisor, the pathologist Dr. Louis Hirsch, did not show up in the laboratory until sometime in the middle of the afternoon. Where could I find donors? The only possible source that came to mind was the men's ambulatory surgical ward on Liholiho I. Surgical patients used to be kept in the hospital for many days after surgery, so there were ten or twelve men in this large post-operative ward. Without authorization, I went there (down three flights of stairs and to the farthest end of the hospital). We had the blood types of the men, and I knew that they were free of infection. So I asked for volunteers, took blood samples, walked back up to the laboratory and cross-matched their blood for transfusion. I had no trouble getting volunteers. Afterward I wondered how I could have done all that I had to do before Helen Carter got there about 10:30—going over to the surgery to draw blood, taking it back to type, going to Liholiho I to draw blood and take back for cross-matching, then taking the report to the surgery. This meant lots of running up and down three flights of stairs and down long halls.

The laboratory staff of technicians included Miss Mabel Slattery, Mrs. Martha Ryerson, Miss Sabina Cummings, Miss Helen Carter, Mrs. Arah Weidman Nieman, Mrs. Mary McCalla and me. Miss Melba Hara was our aide. The orderlies were Kasai, an older Japanese man, and two young Filipino men—Robert and Quirino.

Helen Carter, who lived in Waikiki on the Ala Wai, was the first technician to get to the hospital that day. I don't remember when the other technicians arrived. Helen asked what she should do. I said, "Make up three gallons of normal saline." (We had three one-gallon bottles.) And that was the real beginning of the Honolulu Blood Bank. Blake Clark's book, "Remember Pearl Harbor", reports that Dr. Pinkerton made an appeal for blood donors on radio station KGU at eleven A.M. Citizens of Honolulu began to show up to offer blood. Except for one room that was reserved for emergencies, the Queen's surgery was appropriated for drawing blood. Every day for weeks people stood in line waiting their turn since we supplied all the blood for the military hospitals. According to Dr. Rodney West's book, "Honolulu Prepares for Japanese Attack", the 82nd (1941) Annual Report of The Queen's Hospital reports that during this time the total number accepted as donors was about 4,000, selected from over 5,000 who volunteered to give blood. This activity occupied the entire staff and facilities of our surgeries and laboratory for 16 days, to the exclusion of all other work except the most urgent emergencies.

The blood typing and serological testing were done in our laboratory. The blood from each donor came to us in a glass bottle with two test tube samples attached. One sample was for typing and the other for the serology. We screened all the bloods for syphilis with the rapid, sensitive Laughlin test. All the positives were double-checked by the time-consuming but very accurate Kohlmer-Wasserman method. The glass bottles of blood were stored in three large refrigerators in the laboratory until we had finished the serological testing. All the bloods that tested negative were given to the Red Cross for transport to where they were needed. The positives were discarded and the list of positives given to Dr. Pinkerton to be contacted. Many were not aware of being infected and being infectious. A routine was established so that the questionable bloods could be double-checked the next morning.

Helen Carter continued to work with me to do the serologies. We worked this way for the first critical week going to work at seven in the morning and working until nearly midnight. Since Helen could not go home to Waikiki in the middle of the night, we both stayed at the Harkness Nurses' Home next door for the little sleep we could get. When we finished our nearly seventeen-hour work days, we were escorted to the nurses' home by an armed guard. Since there was no extra room in the nurses' home, Helen and I both had to sleep in my single bed for those first few nights until we reorganized our work to be able to do much of it the next morning.

Helen remembers that on the morning of the 8th we were awakened by the sound of machine gun fire. We both dived out of bed and tried to get underneath the bed. After a few moments, we were laughing at ourselves because only our heads were under the bed; the rest of us up in the air.

Working at night was more than a little bit frightening. The surgery was closed, and Helen and I were all alone on the fourth floor. The pathologist's office and the medical director's office were on a short, open corridor between the laboratory and the open outside corridor where the elevator and a stairway were located. We were quite aware of how vulnerable the island was at that point, and we expected the Japanese to land at any moment. The first night we were told that there was a guard to be stationed at the top of the stairs by the elevator. After working for a time, we went out to see if he was there. He was, but he was asleep. He had been working at Pearl Harbor all day. After that no one showed up.

The laboratory, the pathologist's office and the medical director's office were on one wing of the hospital, and the surgery was on another wing with a connecting hallway. The usually dependable trade winds were the only air conditioning, so all the corridors were on the exterior. The serology workstation was on the side opposite the open entrance, so that we were working with our backs to the door. As a result, Helen and I were vulnerable from three sides—rooftops on two sides and exterior stairs behind us. Night sounds were much exaggerated. The wind rattled the blinds. No light could show, so the first night we were given a flashlight covered with blue cellophane to work by. There was no one within shouting distance. On December 8th our windows were painted black. We then had light at night to work by.

We were alone and working very scared. There was no one within shouting distance to hear us if we called. So we armed ourselves as best we could. At one end of the work table we put a bottle of concentrated nitric acid and an ice pick. At the other end were a bottle of concentrated sulfuric acid and a hammer. And so we worked to exhaustion. One night the pathologist arrived silently in tennis shoes to see if we were actually working late, as we said. We felt his presence and turned around armed. He turned white as a sheet and said he thought he would rather face the Japanese.

The donor line in the hallway outside the surgery was there every morning, people waiting to give blood. In those days there were no disposables. The glass bottles, glass test tubes, calibrated glass pipettes, and the needles all had to be washed clean and sterilized. We used little wire stilettes to push through the needles to be sure that they were kept clear and open. We sharpened our needles on wet stones with great care, before sterilizing, to avoid hurting patients with dull needles.

Only the four major blood groups (A, B, AB and O) had been identified at that time. When a patient's blood could not be successfully cross-matched with a donor of the same type, we had to use an "O" blood. My own blood was such a good, strong group "A" that my serum was used routinely as our typing serum. Things did not come in carefully standardized vials.

Immediately, the morning of December 7th, the Islands were under martial law. The first orders of the military governor were to close the liquor stores and maintain a total blackout of the city. Neighborhood watches were set up. Not so much as a struck match was permitted. All windows had to be covered with black cloth or something to shut in the light. We were required to carry a small gas mask at all times. The covers were very unattractive khaki canvas. In time I made another cover to go over the bag. Mine was navy blue with a red V for victory on the side.

I was able to get downtown to send a cable to my parents on December 9th, telling them that I was safe. We slept with evacuation bags under our beds, though it was very unclear where we could go except perhaps into the mountains. When we heard the sounds of bombs at 2:00 or 2:30 in the morning, we waited tensely for the evacuation alert, thinking that an attempt at invasion was taking place. The military government did not much bother with explanations to civilians.

The beaches all around the Island were ringed with huge rolls of barbed wire. At first curfew was at sunset, and the few emergency vehicles allowed on the streets after dark had their headlights painted a dark blue, with a 2 in. by 1/8 in. slit in each. Ten gallons a month was the allotment of gasoline. Since we had moved to our Happy Home and no longer lived at the hospital, I had a permit to drive at night in case of emergency.

I have kept in touch with Helen Carter, Betty Carpelan and Helen Nieman through the years. These were my special friends and associates during that fearful time.

Helen Carter, an Island girl, married Eric Weiss who was here as an engineer with the Naval Ordnance Laboratories. They lived for many years in Springfield, PA, and now live in Kailua on Oahu. Helen was the first technician to get to the hospital after the attack. Betty Carpelan worked for a time with the Straub Clinic before returning to California where she married Luke McKenzie. Betty who was living in Santa Cruz, California, died October 15, 2002. Betty was the surgical nurse on duty that morning. Helen Nieman, was the first Island girl to win a fellowship to Yale, where she did bacteriological research on Enterococci. She later worked in California where she became familiar with the latest Blood Bank techniques. She returned to Honolulu in the late summer of 1941. Having previously worked briefly in the Queen's lab, she came there the day of the attack and offered her services to the Red Cross. She then went to the Hawaiian Sugar Planters' Experiment Station and used their extensive facilities to design a closed system for the Honolulu Blood Bank. Helen married Lt. Bruce Mac Bride, a Navy pilot, and has continued to live in Honolulu. I, Jane Howe, married Lt. Richard N. Thomas, USNR, in 1945. We lived for years on the island of Maui. I now live in Waikoloa Village on the "Big Island" of Hawaii.

The above account was written especially for the historical record of The Queen's Hospital.

•   •   •

A letter written to my family on February 18th, 1942, has been found which corrects some minor errors in my sixty year old memories:

> "Mother asked a lot of questions about conditions here on December 7th and since and what I saw. I had no time to write at the time, and this seems superfluous since the mainland

newspapers and magazines have undoubtedly given much more vivid descriptions of everything than I would give, even if I could. The first two hours of the war—the actual attack—were very exciting because I didn't know what was going on and wouldn't believe it when I was told.

"I was on duty and doing a pneumococcus typing when I felt the building shaking from the bombs being dropped. I went to the roof-top library, which commands a view from Diamond Head to Barber's Point, including the harbors. I could see the smoke of fires at Pearl Harbor and more smoke in the direction of Hickam Field and Schofield, but the distance is too great to distinguish details. I saw dive bombers fall out of the clouds over the Harbor and lots of anti-aircraft fire. We all assumed that it was "maneuvers" but thought it looked very realistic for any routine stuff. A plane flew near the hospital, which I thought must be perhaps British enroute to someplace else, observing the maneuvers. I made several trips up and down from the roof, trying to get some news and see everything at the same time. When the bomber flew near I coyly ducked under the eaves to hide from the "enemy". I'm glad I wasn't a military objective at that moment.

"Being alone in the lab with only a Japanese assistant and no radio I had difficulty finding out anything. Finally I took the blood-count tray and started around the hospital to get the counts and maybe a little information. Nobody knew anything, but in a few minutes the first casualties started coming in and from then on there wasn't time to consider the meaning of it at all. In fact, the next month is very hazy in my mind. I've no idea the sequence of events or when we learned what little we could believe. Time was suspended. I was at home the Saturday night of the sixth. Betty and I both had a strange feeling of the suspension of time, and discussed it. We looked out at the stars and remarked that we felt somehow hung in a limitless space like the stars. We could not find any reason for the feeling, and then didn't believe the answer when it was given.

"We started taking bloods at Queen's for transfusions and plasma. We handled hundreds a day. Helen Carter and I did the serology on all of them. Since we didn't get the bloods until after they were taken and brought to us, much of our work had to be done at night. The first night was terrifying. (It is far enough away now that I can talk about it without turning clammy.) The windows were not blacked out yet, of course, and we couldn't have any lights on. We did our necessarily close and accurate work by one tiny light covered with blue cellophane, placed under the desk against the wall. I never appreciated anything so much in my life as the dawning of December 8th. The only place I went for two weeks was down to the cable office to send your cable. I was too busy to listen to whatever rumors were undoubtedly in circulation, and I was in effect as isolated as if I had been on top of a mountain.

"I am not enjoying writing this letter to this point.

"Now that we have daylight savings time, pedestrians may be abroad until nine o'clock and cars until 7:30. We can't use our cars very much, however, because gasoline is so carefully rationed. We carry our gasmasks with us always, as well as various forms of identification. I've been fingerprinted several times. In all I have eight or nine different

identification cards and passes. You should see my
picture of the night pass for duty—six for a quarter
passport kind. We can never go anywhere in the
evenings any more. I haven't seen a movie for four or
five months. Shows close at six and eating places at
eight at the latest. And one actually looks twice at a
civilian suit. When letters come with "U.S.A." on
the return address we feel quite disowned, as if we
were no longer part of America.

"Speaking of black-outs . . . . You used to tell
me as a child that one cannot see complete darkness.
Now I tell you that maybe you never have, but I
have. Black-out doesn't mean pulling down the
blinds. It means not a ray of light from dusk to dawn,
with life and activity going on inside the house. It
means being so careful that you think a strip of sky
seen through the porch is the window of someone's
room—and your pulse jumps ten points. It means
seeing the same people for hours every day and liking
them just as well when no one has anything new to
say. As a matter of fact, we talk very little. Four of us
live in one large room here at Happy Home. We go
about our little business without speaking for an
hour or so very often.

"It is such a wonderful pleasure to have our
Happy Home to live in. No matter how upsetting
or hectic the day has been we feel at peace when
we come home, and we come home as fast as ever
we can in the evening. I started a ten week first-
aid course today. It is about time I learned
something about it."

One would think that the memories might dim after these
many years. Somehow this is not the case. They rush back with
terrible clarity, and it seems like only yesterday.

THE WAR YEARS
1941-1945

When did the war with Japan begin? The history books say it began with the bombing of Pearl Harbor on December 7, 1941. I wonder if it began when we started shipping thousands of tons of scrap metal to Japan, which they used to build their ships and planes. They could not have done it without us, since they have few natural resources and no iron mines. From early in 1941 our navy found the Pacific Ocean to be a threatening place because of the Japanese naval build-up. However, we shall start with December.

For my part, I will always believe that President Franklin D. Roosevelt bears the most responsibility for that day that he called "A Day of Infamy". He kept assuring the Pacific commanders that he had everything under control. I also fault Admiral Kimmel for apparently leaving the northern quadrant of the Pacific unpatrolled. If the navy didn't have enough ships and planes to patrol the entire Pacific, why didn't they use army planes? Hickam Field had in training big planes that could fly to Midway Island and back or to Australia. They were there to protect the Islands. Why weren't they used? These thoughts have puzzled me for sixty years.

My recollections, indeed, my knowledge, of the first days of the war are limited to what went on at the hospital. We were so busy that I don't even remember hearing many rumors. It was a couple of days before I could make a hasty trip to the Western Union office and send a cable home to say that I was all right. I had no knowledge of what was going on in the city, what was going on in the Navy Yard or of the situation with the casualties. We were just busy providing blood. There were many civilian casualties cared for at the Queen's Hospital that day, but I was too busy to be aware of any statistical details. I write only of my own experiences as I remember them. In the city there were 57 deaths and more than 300 people injured, mostly, probably, caused by shells from the "friendly fire" from Pearl Harbor and desperate shooting at enemy planes.

Immediately on December 7th, 1941, the Islands were placed under military jurisdiction. The military government appropriated 'Iolani Palace as its headquarters. The palace had been built by King David Kalakaua, who reigned from 1874 to 1891 and oversaw the construction, using the finest of materials including the rare woods of the Islands. The grand staircase to the second floor was made of koa wood and all hand-carved. The throne room was elegantly furnished with the finest of fixtures and with the royal standards on either side of the thrones. This beautiful royal palace was roughly and carelessly used by the military (and required very extensive rehabilitation after the war).

The military governor issued a series of orders for security. Mail was carefully and completely censored, so that letters home contained mostly family chitchat. Blackout was total and monitored by block wardens. Not even a match could be struck outside, and no light could show from inside a house. Everyone was issued a small gas mask, which had to be carried at all times. The Islands were completely vulnerable, and we expected the Japanese to come back and take them any day. The sight of those big, red circles on the underwings of the bombers was indelibly in mind.

The population of the Islands was almost half Japanese who

had been brought here to work in the sugar cane and pineapple fields. Many were American citizens, and of course this included all second-generation Japanese. The Japanese were essential to the economy of the Islands. Only a few who had been carefully screened by the FBI were sent to the camps on the mainland. There was a shocking change in the lives of the local housewives who depended on the help of their maids and housekeepers. Their helpers left for well-paying jobs at Pearl Harbor. We also faced the realization that if (when?) the Japanese returned to take the Islands the local Japanese were in the best position. If the Islands remained American, they were loyal Americans. If the Japanese returned and took the Islands, they would claim to be loyal Japanese. This being the case, we were not quite sure how far to trust their loyalty to the United States. The loyalty of the Nisei (second generation Japanese) was well proven by the very highly decorated 442nd Battalion in Italy.

The Queen's Hospital, where I worked as a laboratory technician, was a focus of activity those first days. As I have stated before, we essentially started the Honolulu Blood Bank by drawing blood from about 5000 donors to send to the military hospitals for the care of the men wounded in the bombing attack, since early efforts to get a blood bank started had not progressed very far. Except for emergencies, the Queen's Hospital surgery was entirely used for taking blood from the volunteer donors who lined up in the hallway every day. At that time it was customary for blood donors to be offered a shot of liquor if they wanted it, to fend off faintness. One wall had cases of bourbon and brandy, available after the military governor closed all the liquor stores. The head surgery nurse tried to keep a bit of a tally. If a donor refused a drink, as occurred occasionally, she made a mark. Before the end of the month, when the rush of obtaining blood for the service men was over, the tally amounted to two bottles of bourbon and a bottle of brandy.

The sixteen surgery nurses and I lived on the second floor of one wing of the Harkness Nurses' Home. It was Christmas, and we were all very tired and very scared. But we had a quiet

Christmas party, and no one bothered us. Betty Carpelan's room was just around the corner from mine. We gathered in Betty's room, sitting around on the floor, thinking of the Christmas celebrations back home and trying not to cry. With determination I had created a Christmas tree by taking a palm branch, cutting it in tree shape and standing it up in a little jar of paraffin. It was trimmed with tiny animals that came in penny candy machines and strips of foil cut from cigarette wrappers. There were of course no Christmas presents. Everything came from the mainland in ships, and ships brought only war materials and necessary food for the first months after December 7th.

In the months before December, Japanese residents were doing much coming and going to and from Japan. The men went "to see their sick mothers". Yasu, a surgery orderly whose family came to the Islands as plantation laborers, came back looking very well. He had obviously been well-fed while in Japan. Yasu then visited each of the other islands and came back wearing leis. Kasai, our rather elderly laboratory orderly, came back from Japan looking very thin and depleted. I noticed this difference at the time, and after the attack it kept coming to mind because Yasu had such a good view of Honolulu Harbor from the surgery windows. It probably did not mean a thing. Lots of people had a good view of the harbor, and his inter-island visits might well have been as a representative of a Buddhist Society or some such, but for some reason I never trusted Yasu. It did not seem to me likely that anyone whose family had come to the Islands as immigrant laborers would have wealthy relatives in Japan. When Yasu came back looking prosperous and had reason to visit the other islands, there were questions in my mind.

Shortly before the war began, I happened to have two or three dates with Navy Lt. "Rosy" Rozinski, who drove a little old blue Model A Ford roadster. Because they were out at sea so much of the time, if a young naval officer had a car it was usually little and old. On December 11th a courier arrived from the Pearl Harbor navy yard with an envelope for me. The envelope contained car keys and a note asking me to take care of the Model

A so that it would be available if he got back to Pearl Harbor. He said that he was leaving for an unknown destination. He did come back two or three times, and the car was available for his use. The civilian gasoline allowance was ten gallons a month, so my use of it was limited.

Life was very different. No more sunny weekend afternoons on the beach. The beaches were all covered with barbed wire. No more dinner dancing in evening clothes, with leis. Curfew was at sunset and strictly enforced. Everyone was off the streets. We were fortunate to have a swimming pool at the nurses' home, so that there was some opportunity for recreation in the sun when we had time.

I had purchased a 1942 calendar designed by the artist, Elsie Das. It was twelve inches square and made of a heavy construction paper in different colors. For each month there was a lovely Hawaiian design. The squares for each day were large enough that I could use it for a diary. I still have the calendar, and it will be a reference for the following account. Because we were so fortunate to have such fine living quarters, it seems appropriate to describe them in more detail.

On January 21st, 1942, the sixteen surgery nurses and I moved into our "Happy Home". Happy Home was a fine old home on Ke'eaumoku Street. A local family had given their parents' estate to the Queen's Hospital. The stone mansion stood on several acres of land. In the front was a formal garden with a fountain. On one side was a grove of trees in which sat a large bronze lion that we liked to sit upon. On the other side was a tennis court in the lower part of the garden, and a blue tile swimming pool with cabañas was on one side of the house. Behind the house was a large area with fruit trees and what had been a vegetable garden. From the front door one entered a foyer with rooms on either side. The central part of the house was a large hall opening to the pool. A double, curved stairway led to the upstairs and was guarded by an imposing bronze eagle. A library, the kitchen and a bedroom and bath were on the other side. There were no furnishings in the downstairs except for a table and a few chairs in the kitchen, which was the only room that was blacked out. The seventeen of us occupied the two upper floors.

Four of us lived in the master bedroom on the second floor. We each had a bed, a dresser and a desk. There was at least one large four-drawer chest. (I'm not sure if we each had one.) The room was so large that we did not feel crowded. Our room was not blacked out at first because there were six huge windows and it was so light and the view was so beautiful we didn't want it all covered with black paper. So we bought a 27-yard bolt of a soft apricot color and made drapes lined with black sateen, which we could draw back in the daytime. Because I made most of my clothes I had a compassionate friend at my favorite fabric shop, Kaimuki Dry Goods, who saved needed materials for me. All of the black fabric had immediately been taken for use by the army, but when more came in my friend had some available for me.

The kitchen was large enough to accommodate several of us at one time. This was good because we usually preferred to come home as soon as we were off duty at three thirty and then fix our own suppers later, rather than to stay at the hospital and wait for the four-thirty dinner hour. Except for some vegetables, which were grown on the islands of Maui and Hawaii, all of our food had to be shipped from the mainland. Some canned meat seemed to be available. So we usually had Spam and Vienna sausage on our shelf. I think these were not available on the mainland. But I could have made a long list of things we did not have or could not find from time to time. We cooked whatever was available. The diary tells of going to market after market to find food, sometimes such basic things as eggs. The diary also seems to say that I made lots of cottage cheese the way my mother taught me. I did not waste much space talking about food in the small diary squares.

House rules were very strict. We appreciated our beautiful home and respected the privilege of living there. Since everyone smoked, we purchased a dozen or so small colored ceramic pots and placed them strategically all about the premises, for extinguished cigarettes. Anyone who threw a cigarette on the grass was not invited back. All entertaining was at the lanai by the pool. The two cabañas provided dressing rooms for the swimmers. It was not possible to black out the vast first floor, and strict, complete blackout was required, and the block wardens kept very careful watch. So we could not entertain inside the house. Beautiful, comfortable year-round Hawaiian weather made all the difference. Entertaining was constant with so many girls living there. With seventeen of us, there was usually a crowd. Early in the war, ships were in and out of Pearl Harbor. At first our Navy friends had to leave by five-thirty in order to get to a bus for Pearl Harbor by black-out time, so there was just time for a swim and a little drink for a relaxing afternoon.

It was quite different being in the hostess position rather than always being on the receiving end of attention. Since I had never bought liquor at a store, one of my most embarrassing experiences was that of obtaining a liquor license. A license was a requirement of the military government in order to buy liquor, and we considered it our patriotic duty to have a relaxing libation available when the men came in from the sea. To get a license one had to be gone from work for several hours, standing in an endless line at the city hall. The line went from the front door across the large foyer and up about fifty steps. Everyone in town was there, the elegant as well as the disreputable.

We were unbelievably fortunate to have such a wonderful place to live as our Happy Home since there were no more weekends going to the beach—the beaches were all covered with barbed wire; no more picnics with only ten gallons of gas a month, which had to be used for going back and forth to work; no more dinner dancing. In fact there was hardly any going out to dinner. At first we had to be back home by sunset—if a taxi could be found with any gas to take us. To have tennis courts and a swimming pool at home, where we could invite our friends, was incredible luxury, and we were jealous to see that nothing spoiled it. Therefore, our house rules were very strict.

Sometimes the men got into port and off duty in time to get something at the liquor mess, very often not. We civilians had a weekly liquor allowance, so every week we bought a bottle of something at the corner drug store. Since all wines, liqueurs and brandies were one price—$1.88, this was not such a hardship. Before our liquor stores were again opened, the navy had champagne available for a time. The officers discovered that a Navy gas mask cover would hold three bottles of champagne. The gas mask covers always arrived full, so there was always some for those who had nothing to bring. When the champagne supply source ran out, there was some in the chest of drawers to help fill the empty period. We tossed the champagne corks and gardenias into the pool to float about in the moonlight.

At the Queen's Hospital I was responsible for doing the blood chemistry tests as well as for the serology. At least one of the tests required 200 proof alcohol for a color change determination. I signed for this in very small amounts from the pharmacy. When the dry spell came I phoned the chemist at the Dole pineapple factory laboratory to inquire about the alcohol they produced. Since the 95% alcohol usually shipped from the mainland for use in sterilizing instruments, etc., was no longer available, pineapple alcohol was being used. It had a very strange odor. My inquiry was to determine the quality and purity of this alcohol. The chemist assured me that it was more pure than the alcohol that had been used. The odor was from esters which they had tried and tried to eliminate, thus making it very pure. Later in the war a "Five Feathers" brand of bourbon was produced from this, esters and all. But my research reassured me that it was safe to use as a libation. And so, for one weekend, a small amount of pineapple alcohol was appropriated for our humanitarian purposes. A little mixed with a lot of grapefruit juice seemed to be somewhat palatable. All of this sounds very boozy, but it was the means we had of making life more bearable for the fighting men. Their lives on shipboard were much, much more restricted than ours. A glass of something cold added to the relaxation, and we were as resourceful as needed to provide this balm.

At one point my roommate, Betty, and I made victory cushions for our long-time friends, Johnny and Arky from the cruiser U.S.S. Portland because they said that the only complaint they had was that their chairs were hard! We covered the cushions with navy blue fabric with large red Vs and with their initials in white. We hoped that our efforts made their duties a little easier— and that they did get to sit down from time to time.

Time seemed to move very quickly—and not to move at all. Because of our extreme anxiety and insecurity, waiting for an invasion by the Japanese, each of us slept with an evacuation bag under the bed, though there were no directions of what to do or where to go in case of evacuation. There was really no place to go. In fact, until after the Battle of Midway was won in June of 1942 we had no feeling of security at all. Tension in the Islands remained very high. Several times we were awakened in the middle of the night by the sound of bombs, and we waited for the evacuation alert which never came. We named the mysterious bomber "*Yehudi*" for no good reason that I can remember, but we were never given an explanation by the military government of what was going on. But of course they never did give out military information.

As the war was moving into the Pacific, we heard about the battles sometimes long after they occurred or when they were reported in the press. But we never knew which ships were involved so we just worried, and prayed for all of them. My diary for the last week in May says that the Big E (the carrier Enterprise) and the carrier Hornet came in from somewhere. The "Sweepea" (the U.S.S. Portland, which was with the carrier group) came in with Arky and Johnny and Whiff aboard. These were the long-time friends we always saw when their carrier group came into port. Arky said he had had ten hours leave in one hundred days. I believe they must have come up from the battle of the Coral Sea. Arky and I had lunch and a swim at Happy Home and we planned a party for the weekend. Saturday came, and no word from the boys. In the afternoon we found that the Portland had gone out that morning. As we later discovered, they were in port for those two days only, just long enough to re-supply the ship, and then off to the Battle of Midway. It is mind-boggling to consider their exhaustion.

Emotionally it is hard, even now, to be reminded and to write about these first days of the war.

On June 3rd the diary says, "Rumors are rife about the Lexington, and Midway has been taken. The Japanese bombed the Aleutians this morning. I could push every rumor down people's throats". And the next day, "Another attack (on the Islands) seems imminent. We moved many things to the basement this afternoon. Restless and rather depressed tonight. People are such fools." On the 6th it says, "Alert is off. Battle of Midway is *pau* (over). Many Navy and Marine flyers lost. Yorktown lost."

Life changed, and it is hard to write about these days. There was fun, but it was bittersweet. There was much forced gaiety as we entertained daily at Happy Home. We felt as if we were doing our "war work" by having the pool parties for any of our friends who were in port and off duty. But there is much sadness at remembering. Life had a very unreal and insubstantial feeling. Everything was topsy-turvy. There seemed to be nothing to which we could hold fast. For the month of January my diary speaks of Arky, Walt, Jim, Norris, James, Bob, Don and Fred. Many of them are just names, with only vague identification in my memory. As our best friends went farther and farther into the Pacific we hoped for mail and wondered if they would ever return. And we had less and less information about what was going on at the time. When the men came in from the sea, they said not a word about where they had been or what they had done, so we had really no conception of what they were going through.

One of the heroes of the war was Lucius Chappell. He was skipper of the submarine that ventured into Tokyo harbor and spent three days there undetected, until he could get his boat out into the open sea again. He married a good friend of mine, later commanded a cruiser in the Mediterranean and retired a Rear Admiral.

Another hero, with whom I had gone dancing two or three weeks before the day of infamy, was Lt. Ted Marshall, one of the very few pilots to get a plane in the air during the attack. A newspaper account reads, "Recognition of a naval aviator's attempt to fight Japanese bombers at Pearl Harbor in planes with which he was unfamiliar was given at ceremonies at the naval air station, where he was presented with a Silver Star medal. The citation told how he had first commandeered a truck and braved machine gun bullets and bomb fragments to drive personnel to battle stations. Later, despite a total lack of experience with land aircraft, he tried a takeoff in a fighter plane that was severely damaged by Japanese fire and unfit for flight. Undaunted, Lt. Marshall rushed to a torpedo bomber and went into the air and pursued enemy aircraft until his depleted fuel supply forced his return to the station." Great dancer, by the way.

Sometime after Midway the curfew time was relaxed, eventually to ten o'clock. The Wai'alae Golf Club clubhouse was turned into a recreation center. Once a month on Sunday evening at the dinner hour the original Hilo Hattie entertained with her comic hula at the Wai'alae Golf Club. She was very good and went on to entertain in New York and on the West Coast, and hers is still a famous name in the Islands.

When the ships were all gone, our guests were from nearby Ft. Shafter or Hickam Field or Wheeler Air Force Base, with an occasional civilian expert in something or other. With Pearl Harbor as home port, some of the ships did come in several times during the summer of 1942. My diary says in September that Arky had received his long-awaited orders to flight school in Corpus Christi, and that he wanted me to go with him. He was such a wonderful person that I wrote, "I almost wish I could see it his way." He had frequently asked me to marry him, but I had enjoyed his company as a very special friend. Actually I had many proposals of marriage from lonely boys, but none were as persistent as Arky. All three of our Portland friends had requested flight training immediately after the December bombing. They seemed to think that being in the air was a superior position. All three got their orders. Arky was in port only one time after he got his wings. Some years later he died of leukemia. Johnny married an admiral's daughter. Whiff retired a captain. Don was my destroyer friend with whom I was a bit in love, in spite of the fact that he was a career naval officer. I did not think I was cut out to be a Navy wife, but Don might have changed my mind. Later there was Harry, but he was soon gone.

Harry came back once. He flew one of those old, slow PBY rescue planes, which had very little instrumentation. He told of a night rescue of a downed pilot when it was so black dark that there was no horizon—the sea and the sky were all the same. He knew he had the angels on his side when he managed to take off in the waves successfully. Harry felt that his survival was as miraculous as the rescue. I do hope he survived the war so that he could practice the alchemy that he wanted to try. Alchemy was the important chemistry of the 4th century B.C. Their theory was that mercury represented spirit and sulfur was soul. One was liquid, and one was solid, and the two held things together somehow. Since gold was the densest of the elements, they thought that they might be able to make gold by making other elements denser. I don't know how Harry planned to accomplish it, but I do hope he had a chance to try.

I had letters from Don, and he came back once. He was very quiet. Afterward I realized that his ship had probably been part of at least one of the horrific night battles in the Coral Sea which involved many ships, when there was no way to tell whether they were shooting at their own ships or at Japanese ships. The night sky was lit by explosives, but there was no way to identify which ships were where. He later wrote that his home port had been changed to San Francisco, and I did not see him again.

As I think of these things, looking back from the first year of the twenty-first century I am looking at a different world. Then it was a Norman Rockwell world. In the first half of the twentieth century, honor and integrity were very important. Character counted. There were absolutes. God was not dead. There was right and wrong. Casual sex was not expected. Drugs were not a problem. And we did not throw trash out of car windows.

I had the idea, innocent perhaps, that so long as I was a lady I could go anywhere in safety. My plans for world travel had been changed by the war, and I will never know whether I could really have made it around safely. But I think I have always had angels to guard me, so it might have been. At least I never had reason to doubt it in my many years in the Islands. Even in such a place as the port city of Honolulu, we did not lock the doors to our houses. We did not lock our cars. We could walk at night without fear. I will never know whether my idea would have worked in other parts of the world. But back to the matter at hand . . . .

Even though we were farther and farther from the war, it was sometimes brought very close. Occasionally the U.S.O. would call me to come and help entertain. Once I was invited to a party at the Ewa Marine Air Station. This was for a group of flyers who had just graduated from college and entered the service. The ones I met were from Ivy League schools—handsome, athletic young men, the cream of American youth. I invited several of them to Happy Home for a swim the next day. Then they were gone. As we learned later, they were on their way to Guadalcanal. The reports soon thereafter indicated that ninety-five percent of the flyers were lost in the first wave of that terrible battle. Our beautiful pool at Happy Home would have been their last happy memory of the good life.

The Chris Holmes mansion in Waikiki housed Navy flyers, and the U.S.O. also called for parties there. Chris Holmes was a wealthy Californian who owned this house and also a beach house on the Pearl Harbor Peninsula. These parties were for navy flyers on short R&R, maybe a week-end or a week. Neither they nor I wanted to think of what they were going through daily on duty, so the thing to do was to concentrate on the party. Reality was too hard to deal with.

The first of the Big Bands to arrive was Artie Shaw's, and Jack Teagarten was one of his players. He played for two tea dances at Fort Shafter before going on farther west. Kirby, a doctor at Tripler Hospital, asked me to both of them. This was wonderful! It seemed a long time since there was any dancing, and I loved to dance.

Other army bases had parties. Two were memorable. The

first one Betty and I were invited to was an afternoon dance at Wheeler Field. My date, a major, was pleasant company. As evening approached, our dates urged us to stay for dinner. At that time I believe curfew was at nine o'clock, and we thought it would be difficult to get home by that time. The major's job involved the use of a staff car, and he assured us that he had passes that would take care of everything. We were talked into staying. After dinner we started in to town. Passing checkpoint after checkpoint, we were waved on through. As we got into town I wanted to take a back street that I thought would be a good idea for more safety. The officers felt so sure of themselves that we went right down the main street.

But not very far, before we were stopped by Police Lt. Yamashiro, ticketed, and taken to the station. There was some emotion involve with our arresting officer having a Japanese name. Of course we knew that we could trust the second-generation Japanese, but again I saw those big, red circles on the bombers. Anyway, off we went to the station to be booked. As we came into the station house, the night clerk growled, "What is this, ladies night?" On one side of the room were two women sitting by the wall who had also been brought in. We were much embarrassed and very angry. Our military protectors were more than a little chagrined. We knew that this meant going to military court and paying a fine or giving a pint of blood. Court was scheduled for the next day at noon. Also it would mean explaining at work, which was not a pleasant thought. We told our "friends" in no uncertain terms that they had better take care of it before the next noon. They did. I suppose they talked to the judge themselves, or asked their superior officer to do it for them.

The other party, at Hickam Field, was an all-day affair. A huge affair. There were pigs being cooked in imu (pits) for barbecue, and extravagant entertainment. A mock volcano was constructed for background. There was Hawaiian music and dancing and Tahitian music and dancing. There was a spectacular fire dance. I believe there were a lot of flyers in from far places or on their way to far places.

Helen Carter, who worked with me during those first fearful days and nights, had a friend, Eric Weiss, an engineer who had come before the war to work in the Naval Ordnance Laboratory. With the onset of the war, the half-dozen engineers were moved from their Waikiki apartments to the Pearl City Peninsula next door to their boss, Doyle Northrup and his wife, Sybil. The engineers next door were in the home of a Japanese who was sent to a concentration camp on the mainland when it was proved that he was an officer in the Japanese Navy. His house happened to have a perfect view of all the ships and of the naval air station at Ford Island. His departure made it convenient for the engineers to have a very comfortable place to live. Every few weeks Mr. Northrup gave his engineers a weekend off, and invited Helen out to the peninsula. She asked me and two other girls to go along. We stayed with the Northrups.

The Northrups lived in Chris Holmes' peninsula house, the other one of his Island homes, besides the mansion in Waikiki. The peninsula house had a tennis court and swimming pool. It also had Dorothy, Chris Holmes' wonderful cook. She fed us and the engineers next door royally each weekend we were there. (When I was married three years later she brought me the gift of a "Joy of Cooking" cookbook. I had always praised her meals, but the gift was a delightful surprise.) Those were wonderfully relaxing weekends for all of us. We dubbed our country estate the "U.J. Ranch" for some reason that I don't remember. We played tennis or swam in the pool—or just did nothing but lie around in the sun. Those were delicious weekends.

A quote from a letter home: "You wondered what I was doing on the 4th of July. I went out to the Pearl City Peninsula for a weekend at the Northrups'. It was about six in the evening when someone remembered that it was the fourth of July so we clapped our hands a couple of times and said, 'BOOM'. There hadn't even been any more gunfire than usual that day. What you really call a quiet fourth. We celebrated by going swimming about ten o'clock and listening to the Mikado which I guess hasn't been censored."

Helen and Eric were married in 1943 and Eric was transferred to Washington, D.C.

Near the end of 1942 there were major changes. Dr. Larsen came back from his heart surgery and asked me to come and help him, and I went to work at the Medical Group. Dr. Larsen needed both a secretary and a nurse. I was neither, but help was scarce. Recruits could not come from the mainland during the war, and having been gone so long he had lost his excellent secretary. So we managed somehow. I revered Dr. Larsen and would do whatever I could to help. He had been so long in the hospital on the mainland that I did things like going out and getting his lunch, and trying to run interference against extra demands on his time and energy. My typing was terrible, but I learned the nursing part easily, and did EKG's and skin testing for allergies as well. Dr. Larsen's interests were wide and his knowledge and foresight incredible. With his new physical limitations he had to give up such things as underwater photography, so he turned to etching and finally to water colors. I was also his art critic. (Here, I jest.) But he graciously treated me as if I were important and shared his pleasure in his art by bringing his pictures for my comments.

While being immobilized in the hospital following his heart surgery Dr. Larsen practiced the art of etching. He could hold the copper plate and stylus in his hands and work without other bodily movement. His colored etching titled "War and Peace" won critical acclaim in the National Physicians' and Surgeons' annual art show and was also the annual gift print for the Honolulu Print Makers. The following is copied from the time of presentation by the Honolulu Printmakers:

> Dr. Nils Paul Larsen, like the physician Sir Seymour Haden, after success in many fields, became interested in the art of etching after the age of forty. Dr. Haden's interest was stimulated by his brother-in-law, James McNeill Whistler. Dr. Larsen's artistic bent was fostered by his close

friend and teacher, John Kelly. He began to study printmaking in 1938 and since that time has received coveted recognition from different sources. He was elected a member of the Society of American Etchers of New York and received honorary mention for a print exhibited by that society in 1941. He has shown his work a number of times with the American Physicians' Art Association where over twelve hundred members exhibited for honors. He received prizes from that organization in the years 1940, 1941, 1942 and 1944.

Dr. Larsen was born in Stockholm, Sweden, and came to America at the age of three. He received his education in the New England public schools, at the Massachusetts State College and at the Cornell University Medical College where he later became instructor in bacteriology and medicine.

His enthusiasms are so diversified that it is hard to list them in a short article. He has contributed many scientific studies published in a variety of medical journals. He has traveled extensively—but all his activities have shown an enthusiasm for man and a faith in the possible progress of man. An artist-philosopher is Dr. Larsen. Throughout his work, whatever the subject matter—flowers, ocean depths or city streets—you will find a record of "human feelings, ambitions, hopes, hates, faith and dreams." And who knows more about those than a physician!

Perhaps his experience in the First World War with the Medical Corps, 106th Infantry as lieutenant, captain, and major gave him the longing for Peace and an additional insight into its meaning. At any rate in this gift print for the year 1944—a sepia version of the color print "War

and Peace" which won a prize from the Honolulu Art Society last year—is shown that subtle claim of fragile beauty raised triumphant against the entanglement and barbed bitterness of war. In years to come the Associate Members will be glad to have this reminder that "The meek shall inherit the earth."
HONOLULU PRINT MAKERS
Alice F. Poole, Secretary-Treasurer
Juliette May Frazer, President

Dr. Larsen gave me one of these treasured gift prints, which shows morning glories growing on the tangled rolls of barbed wire that covered our beaches during the war. He learned his etching techniques from the artist, John Kelly, his good friend and neighbor. Later he worked also in oils and watercolor.

Working with Dr. Larsen was both exhilarating and exhausting. He was used to having such energy that he seemed to have forty-eight hours in every day. Of course he had to resign as medical director of the Queen's Hospital, but he maintained contact with all of his plantation physicians and continued the publication of the monthly *Plantation Health Bulletin*. A letter written to my family on December 12, 1942, reports:

"I have just been typing a paper for Dr. Larsen concerning the further advances in the health progress of the plantations here, even during a year of war. The health conditions and opportunities on the plantations are something that should be advertised everywhere in the world. Even here people are not necessarily aware of it unless they have something to do with plantations. Listen to this put down in words. This is fact, not a nebulous dream of what might be . . . . The common laborer on the plantation is guaranteed work, food, shelter, education, recreational facilities such as theaters and well-equipped playgrounds, hospital facilities, children's clinics, old age and infirmity protection." Dr. Larsen called this treatment of laborers "intelligent selfishness" on the part of the plantation owners. (Some plantation managers were more intelligent than others.)

An article in *Time* magazine on April 12, 1943, is titled "Lesson from Hawaii":

Best health record in the world is that of the 87,000 workers on the plantations of the Hawaiian Sugar Planters' Association. Their infant-mortality rate, prime index of health status, was only 16 infant deaths per 1000 live births last year—enough to make any health officer whistle. When the owners began the medical program in 1929, the rate on a typical plantation was 160.6 among half a dozen nationalities: Filipinos, Japanese, a conglomeration of Hawaiians, Chinese and Caucasians, a sprinkling of Portuguese and Puerto Ricans.

The man at the back of this triumph of paternalism over disease is big, redheaded, Swedish-born Dr. Nils Paul Larsen, Medical Director of The Queen's Hospital in Honolulu, allergist, artist, mountain climber and deep sea diver (until heart trouble recently put a stop to it). Now 53, he went to Hawaii in 1921 as head of the hospital, a job he kept until his retirement last year. In the 1920's the high infant-mortality rate on the plantations shocked him, but he thought the plantations potentially "the finest biological test tubes in the world." He talked the Association directors into establishing a health research center in Honolulu in 1929.

I am still awed in thinking what a privilege it was to work with such a man. It is rather overwhelming to try to describe Dr. Larsen. He was the best heart doctor in town. He was the best internist in town. He was the best pathologist in town. He was the only allergist in town. He studied nutrition and understood about vitamins and trace minerals a generation or so before the medical community began to take notice of their importance. He traveled the world and was decorated by the King of Siam and by the King of Sweden. On one of his round-the-world trips, he took pictures of children's teeth along the way, correlating diet with tooth decay.

Dr. Larsen's patients loved him, and he cared for them—for the whole person. Interesting things would turn up outside his office door. Sometimes there would be flowers. Sometimes fresh fruit or vegetables in lovely Hawaiian ti leaf bundles. Mrs. Lamb, who had a bakery, would come with warm Portuguese sweet bread—fresh from the oven—two loaves for Dr. Larsen and one loaf for me. The artist, John Kelly, was not only a friend and neighbor, but also one of his patients.

Mary Kawena Pukui, the greatest authority on the Hawaiian language and culture, was another whom I was honored to meet.

David Kahanamoku was another. He was one of four Kahanamoku brothers who formed a winning Hawaiian swim team in four successive Olympics. David was chosen by the scientists who developed the Hall of Man in the Field Museum in Chicago as the perfect Polynesian. His statue in bronze, with his ten or twelve foot wooden surfboard stands in the Hall of Man. He told me of his experiences during the preparation for the statue. The scientists who chose him put him in a full plaster of Paris cast—and then went to lunch while it set, leaving him entirely alone. He felt as if he would have died if he had not expanded his lungs to their fullest extent. It was a horrifying, almost unbearable, experience.

I was much interested in Dr. Larsen's theories about allergy (or atopy, as he sometimes called the phenomenon). I had made vaccines using house dust from the patient's own home, or dander from the family dog or cat when I worked at the hospital. Now I was doing the scratch tests on patients' arms to check for the causes of asthma or hay fever, and giving injections of vaccines to alleviate the symptoms. I learned all I could, and at Dr. Larsen's behest wrote a paper on "Atopy" to present to the Hawaiian Academy of Science. None of the doctors there knew what I was talking about or paid any attention, but I suppose it is on file somewhere in the annals of the Academy. It was several years before another medical clinic sent a doctor to the mainland to learn about allergies and their effects.

One of Dr. Larsen's hobbies was underwater photography, at which he was expert—as he was in everything he did! When the premier expert in underwater photography came from Hollywood to the Islands to do some work. Dr. Larsen invited him to dinner, and I happened to be invited also. After dinner the slide projector was turned on, and the visitor asked to show some slides of his work. After he did this, he asked Dr. Larsen to show some of his own work. Since Dr. Larsen's work was so far superior, the comparison was quite embarrassing. Since Dr. Larsen could no longer practice his hobby because of his health, the "expert" must have been relieved.

My friend Betty also left Queen's and went to work for another of the local clinics, so we found an apartment to rent on Dominis and Makiki Streets, very near Happy Home. It was hard to leave Happy Home—it was such a lovely, comfortable place to live.

Some time in 1944 I had a note from Rosy Rozinski from the West Coast saying that he would not be back to Pearl Harbor. I was authorized to sell the car if I wanted. I did, to the relief of the doctors at the Medical group, who thought it did not look very appropriate parked next to their beautiful cars. That meant taking the bus to and from work. The buses came through the downtown area before getting to the Medical Group, and I waited for as many as ten buses to pass me by, already filled. That was quite a negative. However, I now had a private telephone number in my own apartment.

Enter the architects. Several aspiring young Honolulu architects were classified 4F in the military draft and did not serve in the armed forces. They did their war work at Pearl Harbor. Some organization had a big get-acquainted get-together for civilians. I believe it was held at the Central Union Church. With all of the Navy gone, social life was much less active. Whether it was by invitation or not, I don't remember, but I went. Some of the architects were there and I happened to meet them. They were a fun bunch, and I started dating one of them. They all had apartments in Waikiki near the Ala Wai canal. The only one who was married lived just around the corner from the one I dated. So on special occasions, such as a moonlight dance at the House Without a Key at the Halekulani Hotel, I could sleep at their apartment.

The House Without a Key was a pavilion without walls, covered for protection against possible rain, and the dances were only for guests of the hotel. One of the architects lived in one of the hotel cottages. We were his guests for cocktails and had dinner at the hotel before the dance, which happened only on full moon weekends. The best of the Hawaiian "music boys" played their instruments, and the best of the hula dancers entertained there on the beach in the moonlight. It was paradise indeed. It was also quite illegal to be on the street after curfew, subject to arrest and fine. At midnight my date and I made our way stealthily for several blocks to get to the apartments near the Ala Wai, he to his and I to the married couple's couch. Luckily, we were not caught.

Several of the architects were sailors and had their small sailboats in Kewalo Basin. Early on, no sailing was permitted. Eventually restrictions were relaxed to permit sailing only in the Basin. It was necessary to get a fishing license with mug shot and fingerprints to be permitted to sail. I liked to go along for the ride, so I had a mug shot with the rest. For five dollars a year we each had a key to the Honolulu Yacht Club boathouse. The sailors formed the "Rock and Roll Sailing and Chowder Club" and raced for the "Mocha Cup". I made club pennants to fly on the mast of each boat. The Mocha Cup award consisted of a tall wooden base on the top of which stood a teacup with a spoon in it.

The only married couple, Janet and Pete, sometimes visited an officer friend at Wheeler Air Force Base, and I went along a time or two. The officer lived near a pool, and liked a swim after getting off duty. However, he was very tired of having nothing but uniforms to wear, so he had a Japanese seamstress make up some *muʻumuʻu* such as the ladies who sold leis used to wear. These were simple, long, loose garments—very comfortable. He would put on one of these after a swim, and he had others for guests to wear. Pete thought this was a splendid idea, and had muʻumuʻu made for himself and one for Janet. He could sometimes be seen on the streets of Waikiki in muʻumuʻu and *zori* (Japanese slippers). Although anything could be seen on the streets of Waikiki, this had to be one of the most interesting. The *haole* did not wear muʻumuʻu, certainly not the men.

On most weekends one of the architects hosted a party for the crowd. The most outstanding of these came about when one of their number was to be married. Janet and Pete decided on a muʻumuʻu party, to be a surprise to the engaged couple. Everyone was instructed to come in muʻumuʻu, so I made one for my date and one for myself. With the cooperation of a lovely lady at the Kaimuki Dry Goods store, I also made "formals" for the guest couple. The groom's was of black sateen, with a tucked shirtfront of bright pink that buttoned to the black fabric at the bottom. Bright pink stripes replaced the satiny stripes of pants. The bride's was of white sateen with a ruffle at the high neck and cuffs. Narrow blue ribbon made trailing bows at the neck and sleeves. Everyone was present when the couple arrived. We had some apprehension about their reaction. The bride was quite a controlled person, and we wondered whether she would indeed enter into the spirit of the party. She cooperated completely and happily, and even took her muʻumuʻu with her on their honeymoon.

Since it was several years before mu'umu'u began to be worn generally by haole ladies, we were real trendsetters to jump-start this wonderful custom.

I remember that there was a professor at the University of Hawaii whose mother was a friend of my mother. I think she had come for a visit when she was caught by the war. She found an apartment in Manoa Valley and went to work as "housemother" in the bachelor officers' quarters at Ford Island. One flyer kept telling her how much he missed home-cooked food. Finally he asked if he could bring some friends to her apartment and cook some spaghetti. He said he was a very good spaghetti cook. She agreed, and offered to see if she could find some girls to come along and share. She called me. I was not the least bit interested in this plan. I was war weary, but since I felt somewhat guilty for not having done much to acknowledge her presence in the Islands I said that I would try to find some others. My friend Betty and two of the girls from Happy Home agreed to join in.

When the appointed day arrived, the one man who had a car had been called to the mainland and there was no transportation for them or for us, so they came in by bus. It was about two miles from our house to the party, and we tried to find a taxi, but since it was the end of the month no one had any gas left. Betty and I had no food in the house because the next day was market day, and we were hungry. We four girls walked to Punahou Street to catch the Manoa Valley bus. When we got off the bus, we were met by several of the men.

A very tall officer came up to me and walked down the hill with me. He said his name was Dick Thomas. When we got to the house I went to the kitchen to encourage the cook. I was there to eat and to fulfill a perceived social obligation, not to meet someone new. On occasion I would look into the living room, where Betty was sitting beside Dick. His big, brown eyes were focused on me. I thought he was about the most beautiful man I had ever seen, though I really preferred blondes or redheads. At serving time I was designated to sit by the cook. As we sat

down, Dick came up and said, "I'm sitting here", and sat down
beside me.

The Manoa Valley bus did not maintain a late schedule, so
when it was time to go home Dick walked with me the two
miles or so. I had on new shoes, and my feet really hurt. On the
way he told me that he was the replacement for the officer who
went to the mainland. He had not wanted to come but had
acceded to the pleas of the housemother. He said that he was
born in San Francisco, grew up in Riverside, California, and was
a graduate of the California Institute of Technology. After
graduating in civil engineering, Richard worked first as a building
inspector for Los Angeles County, then in the design department
of the Lockheed Company before volunteering for the Naval
Reserve. He received three months of specialized training before
being assigned to duty on the Naval Air Station, Ford Island, in
Pearl Harbor. When the John Rodgers airport (now the Honolulu
International Airport) was built, it became the Naval Air Station.
He was classified as a naval reserve officer; one of those they
called "ninety-day wonders". In his three months of specialized
training before receiving his commission he was sent to the
Massachusetts Institute of Technology and then to Pratt and
Whitney Engine School . . . .

The next night he telephoned. And the next. And the next.
And the next . . . .

I continued to enjoy the social life of the architects for a
while, but finally realized that I was definitely, hopelessly caught.

Now there was another change of scenery. By this time, Pearl
Harbor provided the support for the war in the Pacific. Especially,
it was the way station for planes coming and going. The base of
this operation was moved to the new John Rogers Naval Air
Station (now the Honolulu International Airport), and life
became more organized for the service men. Famous actors staged
plays in Roosevelt High School auditorium. Bob Crosby's band
came to play for dances at John Rogers, where Dick was stationed,
and at the Navy base at Kaneʻohe on alternating Saturday nights.
My friend, Helen Nieman, who had grown up in Honolulu,

married Lt. Bruce MacBride, who was stationed at Kaneohe. The four of us went to all the dances. The men were in white uniforms again, instead of just working khakis. Before the war the men wore tuxedos for dinner dancing in the city, but now "whites" were the dress uniforms for parties on the bases. Navy whites are at least as handsome as tuxedos.

Dick's job description was Maintenance Dispatch Officer for N.A.T.S.—the Naval Air Transport Service. He was responsible for checking the maintenance schedules for the big planes that carried supplies of all kinds to the war area. The planes got bigger and bigger (the B-29 was the biggest) and left so loaded with parts of machinery and one thing and another that they could scarcely take off. Once I was in the street when one went directly overhead. The wings covered the sky from the building on one side of the street to the building on the other side of the street. The planes could barely clear low Diamond Head Crater in the ten miles from the airport. When Dick would call in the evening I would hear a plane take off through his phone, and minute later hear it go overhead. And so the war wore on.

Since my father was a Presbyterian minister as well as an educator, I grew up in that denomination. There were no Presbyterian churches in Honolulu so it was my custom to attend Central Union Congregational Church or St. Andrews Episcopal Cathedral. It was my first introduction to the Episcopal service, and I liked the depth and dignity of the liturgy. With my very busy social life I was not very regular in attendance through the years, though my Christian faith was always the foundation of my life. Being a woman, I have felt a strong allegiance to Jesus as my Lord, since it is only in Christian countries that women have freedom. For this I am very grateful. Dick had grown up with the Episcopal liturgy and was not comfortable with the Congregational service. So when he was free on Sunday we usually attended the service at the Cathedral.

On April 28, 1945, Lt. Richard Notley Thomas, U.S.N.R., and Jane Edythe Howe were married by the Rev. Henry P. Judd at the Church of the Crossroads in Honolulu. Betty Carpelan was my attendant, Lt. Bruce Mac Bride was best man and Dr. Larsen gave me away. For myself I made a long dress of white crepe, with a square neck, long sleeves and a shirred bodice, and wore a short veil. For Betty I made a dress of pale pink. My bridal bouquet was of white orchids from the Atherton collection. We had a wedding dinner at the Halekulani Hotel and a weekend honeymoon at the Kona Inn on the Big Island of Hawaii. Betty moved out of our apartment and Richard moved in. It was all very wartime simple.

The war ended in August and Richard was separated from the Navy in November. He maintained his naval reserve status and retired Commander in 1960. He received no monetary remuneration for his years of service after he left active duty, but served his country freely and proudly. On November 11, 1945, we moved to the Island of Maui, to take up residence in East Maui, called the "Ditch Country". Richard's new job was as resident engineer for the East Maui Irrigation Company, an Alexander and Baldwin Company. E.M.I. served the two large sugar plantations in the valley of Maui, keeping them supplied with water for irrigation.

LIFE IN THE
DITCH COUNTRY
1945-1949

"Ditch Country". Such a name for one of the most beautiful places on earth. The Island of Maui in the Hawaiian Islands is composed of 10,000 ft. *Haleakala* (the House of the Sun)—a dormant volcano, a central valley and the West Maui Mountains. Haleakala rises from the floor of the Pacific Ocean to form the main part of the Island. The wide central valley is fertile, sunny and good for growing sugar cane, but the rainfall is quite inadequate. The trade winds blow from the northeast, and when the clouds come up against Haleakala they drop their water—tons of water. The eastern slope is a succession of breathtaking big and little water-sculpted canyons locally called "gulches". (Gulches indeed!) These have been carved over many eons in the lava which forms the volcano. The ditch country is the rain forest of East Maui.

"Ditch" refers not to the gloriously luxuriant gorges cut by the daily, often torrential, rains that the trade winds bring to the eastern slope of the mountain but to the series of irrigation ditches that nurtures the 35,000 acres of sugar cane in the dry valley. The construction of these irrigation ditches, tunneled through the mountains, crossing the canyons with flumes, tells an exciting adventure story of an amazing engineering feat.

The history of the construction of the first East Maui irrigation ditch is legendary. Two pioneer sugar planters had plantations in the broad valley between 10,000 ft. Haleakala and the West Maui Mountains. Once in geological time these were two volcanic islands born from the "hot spot" whose eruptions from deep down under the sea formed all of the Hawaiian Islands. The older islands have drifted to the northwest, and there is a new one forming under the sea southeast of the "Big Island" of Hawaii. East Maui is the flank of Haleakala.

The two sugar planters were Samuel T. Alexander and Henry P. Baldwin. By 1876 Mr. Alexander was managing the Alexander and Baldwin Plantation while Mr. Baldwin managed the Haiku Plantation. These eventually became one 35,000 acre plantation, the Hawaiian Commercial and Sugar Company. Since rainfall in the valley is light and sugar requires so much water to be produced, they needed to find some way to bring water from the rainy east side into the valley. Mr. Alexander devised a daring plan to build a ditch 17 miles long into the rain forest. This was the Hamakua Ditch.

East Maui was mostly unexplored, watered by the daily rains, which the trade winds dump against the whole side of the mountain. Through eons of time these rains have cut huge gashes in the volcanic rock, forming rugged canyons all along the mountain. Even to find a way to walk along the mountain was a daunting task. Even more onerous, water had to be brought from high enough on the mountainside that it could flow by gravity to reach the dry valley. A lease was obtained from the king, which stated that if the work was not completed in two years the land would revert to the crown. Even though he had lost one arm in a mill accident only a few months previously, Mr. Baldwin dared to undertake the construction of the ditch.

The work progressed with difficulty, catching water from the many waterfalls in the canyons in ditches, tunneling through the lava from one canyon to the next, crossing the gulches with inverted siphons. Mr. Baldwin found the two-year deadline hard to meet, especially having only unskilled labor available. Another complication added to the tension. Their long-time rival, Claus Spreckles, came back to Maui from California with a plan to build an even longer ditch. He talked King Kalakaua into giving him the water rights if Alexander and Baldwin did not finish on time!

The greatest challenge was crossing Maliko Gulch, many hundreds of feet deep. The plan was to use an 1,100 ft. inverted siphon. To put this in place required going down the precipitous sides and back up again, lowering themselves by rope. This was such a dangerous undertaking that Mr. Baldwin did this first every day himself to keep his workers encouraged—even though he had only one arm—until the job was completed. It was a real race against the deadline, but they won! This story of grit and determination forms the foundation for the successful sugar industry in Hawaii. One ditch after another was added until there was the capability of bringing as much as 450 million gallons of water a day to keep the sugar growing.

Eventually there were four large ditches and six others. The main ditch, the Koʻolau Ditch, had 57 miles of ditch and tunnels. Humorous names were given to some of the gulches, as, Puohokamoa, "Frightened Chicken". Someone in this area raised chickens, and an avalanche came and frightened them. And Puaʻakaʻa, the "Rolling Pig". One day a wild pig was crossing the stream in the gulch when a sudden heavy rain higher up the mountain brought gushing water that caught the pig and rolled him down the stream. In Waikamoi, the largest of the gulches, several beautiful waterfalls could be seen from the road. This is the only gulch that extends all the way to the top of Haleakala, and it often carries torrents of water down to the sea.

• • •

When we were there the steep walls of the canyons were covered with a drapery of ferns, shrubs, flowering trees, vines, yellow and white flowering ginger, with many cascading waterfalls. The air always seemed fragrant, whether with the fragrance of green growing things or of flowers. The sugar plantations in the valley depended on water from East Maui being carried in the irrigation ditches to grow the sugar—two thousand pounds of water to make each pound of sugar. The economy of the Islands depended largely on sugar, which was grown on all the major islands. Therefore maintenance of the ditches was a real priority.

Haleakala is designated as a dormant volcano. There is a crater at the summit with a circumference of twenty-one miles and a depth of three thousand feet, with thousand-foot cinder cones rising from the floor. These are quite colorful, with shades from sand to rose. There is a good highway to the summit and on a clear day the Island of Hawaii may be seen to the southeast. Across the crater there are two great gaps, through which the lava poured to make the easternmost part of the island.

There are many legends telling of the miraculous feats of the Hawaiian gods. The four chief gods were *Ku*, *Lono*, *Kane* and *Kaneloa*. King Kamehameha the Great, who conquered the armies of all the other Islands, worshipped the god *Ku*. There were many lesser gods and goddesses. The *ali'i*, the kings and chiefs, traced their ancestry back to one of the four chief gods. There were many lesser gods, worshipped by the common people as protectors, often related to occupation (fisherman, farmer, hunter). The demi-god *Maui* lived in the central valley of the island of Maui. Many wondrous feats are attributed to him. In one, he made the sun stand still so that his mother could get her work done. The story goes:

> Maui lived with his mother, Hina, who had so much to do that she could never quite finish the day's work. The farmers didn't have time to care for their crops, the fishermen couldn't catch enough fish, and none of the women could get all their work done. The *hala* leaves had to be selected

and prepared for weaving the mats. The *kapa* (tapa) had to be pounded into cloth.

Making the kapa was such a lot of work. Hina had to peel the bark from the branches of the *wauke* (mulberry) trees, soaking them to make the bark peel easily. The kapa is made from the soft inner bark. She pounded the wet bark on a board until it was in thin sheets. Then she pounded the sheets together to make cloths for blankets and *lava-lava* (skirts), and *malo* (loin cloths) for the men.

Maui told his mother that he was going to make the sun slow down. He tried several methods, but none of them worked. Finally he made sixteen cords of the strongest fiber and tied them together. Then he took some of his sister's hair and wove sixteen nooses and tied one of them to each of the sixteen cords. The sun was very strong, but he got up very early and went to the top of the mountain, Haleakala. He hid in a little cave until the first leg of the sun came over the top of the mountain. He snared each leg in one of the nooses and held on to the cords. Finally all sixteen of the sun's legs were snared. The sun begged to be set free, but *Maui* made him promise to go more slowly, to the great comfort of all the people.

This was only one of the great feats of the god *Maui*.

● ● ●

Little did I dream when I married my handsome Navy Lieutenant on April 28, 1945, that I would soon be a pioneer housewife, living in that rain forest, miles from civilization, cooking in a fireplace and drying clothes on a rack in front of a fire. World War II ended in August. Of course, I had been in Hawaii throughout the war and chose to live there. Richard also thought that was a fine idea. (Everyone called him "Dick", but I prefer his beautiful name "Richard". Sometimes he will be referred to one way, sometimes the other.)

When an offer came from the East Maui Irrigation Company (E.M.I.) to supervise the maintenance of the miles and miles of tunnels and irrigation ditches, he accepted it. The pay was the same as his lieutenant's stipend, which did not seem like much since I was making an equal amount with my job in Honolulu. But we would not have the expense of city living, the work sounded interesting, and it was an entry into plantation life.

So, when Richard was separated from the Navy in November, we prepared to move from our furnished apartment in Honolulu to a completely unfurnished house at the edge of the rain forest in East Maui. Besides chairs and tables and beds, we needed a stove and refrigerator. Opportunities for these things did not abound, since household goods were not a priority during the war. We searched until we found a householder who had moved with his own furnishings to a "furnished" house belonging to people who had gone back to the mainland. These extra furnishings proved to be just odds and ends which the new householder had stored in his garage, but the necessary stove and refrigerator were both included. Having little choice, we bought the furnishings from the descriptions given and had them shipped to Maui.

The company-owned irrigation supervisor's house which was waiting for us was situated just above the narrow, winding, unpaved road that ran from the central valley (civilization) to Hana at the easternmost tip of the island (the end of the earth). Sometimes the Hana road runs along the precipitous edge of a cliff above the ocean before it winds down to the bottom of the canyons. It *was* very treacherous. In the very early days the road went only as far as Kailua. In 1923 the road was extended to Hana. Until then, travel beyond Kailua was on the E.M.I. Trail on foot or by mule or horseback.

Our house was at the edge of the rainy area, where the rainfall averaged one hundred twenty-five inches a year. Ten miles farther along the road toward Hana the rainfall is about two hundred and fifty inches, and up the mountain from there it is between four and five hundred inches a year. This may, in fact, be the wettest place on earth. The top of 5,208 ft. Mount Waiʻaleʻale on the island of Kauaʻi is said to be the wettest, but no one has gone above the highest of the ditches to check the rainfall farther up on Haleakala. Since rainfall increases with elevation, who knows how much rainfall there may be farther up on 10,000 ft. Haleakala. Cascades of water rush down to the ocean through the many canyons every day. By contrast, in the valley between Haleakala and the West Maui Mountains the rainfall averages about twenty five inches a year. And on the westernmost side the average is about five inches. All this variation occurs within a few miles.

At the end of a narrow lane up the hill from the main road, our house looked down past little Huelo church to Kailua Bay, a little gem of a bay for which the area is named. Our front yard seemed to go down to the ocean; and our back yard to the top of the mountain. We were essentially alone, with no near neighbors except the day laborers. The patio of the U-shaped house was planted with strange ginger plants of varieties unfamiliar to me, and other tropical flowers. The fence behind was festooned with blooming yellow alamanda vines.

The house had been made ready for us with fresh paint, but the meager furnishings we bought sight unseen consisted only of one double bed, two odd twin-size beds, one headboard and footboard, a dresser, a simple chest of drawers, two upholstered chairs in rather sad condition, and that's about all. They needed a lot of help to make a livable home. Fortunately, I did have my beautiful carved teakwood chest to add some style and grace. So, we had the Honolulu Planing Mill make an unfinished rectangular table and six simple chairs with loose seats, to be covered. I don't remember the cost of the table, about $20, I think, and the chairs were $1.50 each. I purchased drapery fabric for the living room and upholstery fabric to re-cover the two chairs and fabric to cover the six dining chairs. A helpful friend gave me a how-to upholstery book and a little upholstery hammer. Everything else was up to me, and I set to work with a will. The dining room furniture was varnished, the draperies made and a fairly credible job done on the upholstered chairs.

Large plants on either side of the teakwood chest were the rest of the living room furnishings until we found out about the abandoned army camp down the road where there was a good gaming table. It was about forty-five inches in diameter with a ledge on the edge for drinks and chips. My husband sawed the ledge off rather roughly. I sanded it smooth and put about a dozen coats of paint on it before getting a nice, smooth finish and the exact shade of dark green that I wanted for a coffee table in the living room. We had several pictures of original art which I had purchased or been given, and I purchased a large piece of canvas to make a pastel wall hanging to go by the fireplace. Imagine!! A fireplace in Hawaii!

Shortly before we moved I had learned that I was pregnant, so the next order of business was the furnishing of the nursery. A baby bed was loaned to us, and we found a small chest of drawers. Two orange crates with a board across between them made a table for bathing and dressing. This board and the bed were painted a soft yellow, and the orange crates were hidden by blue fabric appliquéd with giraffes. A cutout wooden giraffe, also painted yellow and with a lei around his neck was designed to hold towels or clothing. The nursery was made ready.

In a letter to my family I describe our first Christmas in our new country home:

> "Don't worry about a new baby in the tropics, Mother. This is no more so than Southern California. I've been wearing socks and a sweater all day lately, and sleeping under two blankets. The Islands grow fine children. There is no malaria. There are no snakes, no tropical diseases, lots of sunshine and vitamins. It really is a lovely place in which to live.

"We had our first Christmas tree in our house with a fireplace. The fireplace is a great pleasure, and we need it in the evenings. The only decorations I had were one string of lights and some silver icicles. The rest of the breakables I left with Betty in Honolulu, and there weren't any here to buy. (It is still too close to the war.) So I had to make them. It was fun, and it really is quite a satisfactory tree. Richard got it down the road. It looks like a spruce and smells nice. We also have real English holly and Hawthorne from the E.M.I. manager's yard, and also some cedar branches for decoration.

"On the Sunday before Christmas we went to 'Daisy's church', the Huelo church a few miles from here. Mrs. Daisy Kala'upa is a sweet, big Hawaiian woman who has taken charge of the very lovely little church here in the country. I'm not sure whether she is ordained. She is quite a wonderful woman, I think. She speaks sort of a mixture of English and Hawaiian. The program started with the children's part which lasted about 45 minutes, and went into an hour and a half morning service, with the children on the stage all that time! It was an excellent program, especially the music. Hawaiians have beautiful voices. After the service there was a lu'au in the parish house next door."

•   •   •

Daily living was a challenge. The house must have been built by five-foot carpenters. The kitchen counters and sink were at just the right height for them, but not so convenient for us. I was five feet six and Richard was six feet four inches tall. Our back yard held papaya trees and bananas, and wild guavas grew in profusion across the way. All other groceries came from the central valley. Every Friday Fred Wilhelm took his pick-up truck in to the Pa'ia Store to get groceries for the week for all the families in the "E.M.I. Kailua camp." For us this meant everything—bread, milk, butter, eggs, meat, vegetables, sugar, flour, coffee, tea— everything. (No ice cream of course.) To order the groceries I would call the Pa'ia Store and discuss possibilities with the grocer and the butcher. The butcher was wonderful and offered suggestions. He would also hang beef just to our liking! (There are advantages to country living.) However, if I forgot to order anything we didn't have it until the next week, since the company vehicle was all we had at first. Eventually we planted a small vegetable garden.

Bread was a real problem. White "air bread" was the only kind to be had. After a week, sandwiches made with it left much to be desired. Because my mother had liked to bake bread I had an idea about how to handle dough. However, there was no yeast available in the market. We discovered a can, a very old can, of dry yeast in the army camp, and I set to work to do the best I could with it. My bread was better than the air bread. By the time that yeast was used up, cakes of live yeast became available and I became quite expert at white bread, wheat bread, cinnamon bread, raisin bread, cinnamon rolls, and coffee cake.

And cookies! Cookies became important. People on the plantation, knowing that we were living out there in such isolation, felt sorry for "poor Jane". Only in necessity did anyone travel that terrible Hana road. So every one who did travel to Hana made sure to stop. Somehow it always seemed to be at lunch time or tea time. Tea time was easy, since I always had cookies. Lunch time was a bit different, since my weekly planning did not know how to take that into consideration. However, we managed. And it was good to see people and get to know them that way. The best count was twenty four visitors in one month. Why all those people were going to Hana, I can't imagine. There must have been more than one or two in some of the cars. Perhaps they just liked my cookies.

Because of the customary daily rains, occurring usually in the early mornings and in the evenings, there was very little dust. The world appeared fresh-washed, with shining foliage and blue, blue sky above the deep blue of the ocean. Nor was there much mud on the road or on the paths I took on my daily walks. Free dirt had long since been washed away along my path. However, the workmen going up into the forest said "You can forget your lunch pail, but don't forget your raincoat and rubber boots!"

With an irrigation company weather is always of critical concern. So Dick became a volunteer weather watcher. During World War II the Navy pilots who flew regularly across the Pacific noticed that the storms always moved from east to west. After the war, increasing attention was given to the weather patterns across the country, with volunteer observers in all locations and climates. On Maui, with such extreme variations in rainfall, there was an observer on the wet side, one on the dry side and one in between. At our house a barometer was placed on the desk in the office, a rain gauge was installed, and an anemometer placed on the roof of the garage. At six o'clock in the morning and six o'clock in the evening the type of clouds, the barometric pressure, the wind speed and the amount of rainfall were recorded, and the report phoned in to the Kahului airport. In time we saw the pattern of approaching storms.

When I was on my way to the Islands my brother had given me a little silver alarm clock. It sat by our bedside to get us up so that I could fix breakfast while the weather report was in progress. With the approach of a storm the clock began to run slow, which gave us some concern about its dependability. When it was to be just a little storm it slowed down just a little bit. When it was a strong storm it began to slow down two or three days before the storm arrived. We were able to predict the severity of a coming storm by the amount the clock slowed down. After the storm passed, the clock was reset and ticked away at the proper rate. With one big storm it stopped altogether, and we finally had to get a new clock.

Electricity was sometimes a real problem. We were connected

with the valley by an electric wire hung from one "gulch" to the next. Not infrequently a hard storm would break the wire, and we would be without lights, stove or refrigeration. This usually seemed to happen on a week-end just after Fred had brought our meat and groceries for the next week. It might take two or three days before the break in the line could be located, so many a meal was cooked in the fireplace. This was not something I looked forward to with much pleasure. All the meat had to be cooked, of course. I can't remember how I managed to cook the vegetables, but I did wish for a proper hook for a kettle, built into the fireplace. No baking was possible. Somehow what has to be done gets done.

Those were the days when our telephone was a rather heavy black object that sat on the office desk. It had a rotary dial. A receiver was cradled on the top, connected by a cord. Most numbers on Maui were four digits and all calls went through the area operator. Our operator was in Hana, the village farthest from the central valley and the only one of any size in East Maui. This operator was a most accommodating lady who could hear all conversations and so knew the whereabouts of almost anyone at any time, as well as many other matters of personal interest. After a new telephone system had eliminated the operators sometime after we moved in to one of the sugar plantations in the central valley, (the Hawaiian Commercial and Sugar Company), I wondered how folks from Pa'ia to Kaupo could manage without this valuable center of information.

The frequent storms had another interesting effect. Our water supply came right out of the irrigation ditch. With normal conditions the ditches flowed with clear water. With the torrential rains that occurred from time to time the water was muddy. The water reserve was the entire side of the mountain, closed off somewhat above the road, behind locked gates, so that no vehicle could pass unless the driver had keys to the gates. The ditches originate in the canyons which carry the water from higher up on the mountain. The forested mountain seemed so pristine and pure that I actually never worried about drinking the water. But

I learned to drink water from the hot water tank, which at least had allowed for some settling of the muddy water after a hard rain. Times have changed, and I wouldn't trust the many tourists wandering around to respect the locked gates. Now I would not think of drinking the water without boiling it first.

The East Maui Irrigation Company system still includes 74 miles of ditches and tunnels, accessed by 62 miles of private roads, some cut along sheer cliff sides. There are also several difficult walking trails where roads are not feasible. The ten ditches in the system, originating in canyons to catch the water from higher up on the mountain, can deliver as much as 450 million gallons of water a day to the plantations in the wide, dry valley.

The men who worked with my husband were Hawaiian, Portuguese, Japanese and Filipino, reflecting the variety of workers who had been brought to the Islands as laborers. Perhaps because of the beauty of their surroundings, they were gentle people. Or perhaps it was just the influence of the Hawaiians. Richard Thomas was sometimes carelessly over-emphatic in his language. One day he came home and noted humbly that he was the only one who ever spoke that way. He never did again. He became ever more appreciative of the wisdom and insight of the Hawaiians and valued their friendship. We came to love and respect this beautiful land they knew so intimately.

The daily work of maintenance took the men somewhere on the mountainside along the seventy-four miles of ditches and tunnels. And so Richard explored all along the lower part of the magnificent mountain. A favorite week-end pleasure was to go to see one of the exquisitely beautiful spots which had been found during the week's work. I can see some of them in my mind's eye now. At first these delightful trips were taken on Sundays. Richard would come across places of incomparable beauty during the week as he traveled about the mountain. On Sunday we would take a picnic and wend our way in the Jeep up some tiny, little road to a remote spot so pristine that we had the awed feeling the no one had ever been there before. The feeling was a breathless sense of wonder, as if the mysterious mountain were sharing this secret place with us alone. I return to these places in memory with a haunting feeling of unreality.

One of Dick's work crew, David Kahoʻokele, a fine Hawaiian man and a good friend, told us something about his family. They were entrusted with the oral history that was passed down from generation to generation. Genealogy was very important to the Hawaiians. It is said that the highest chiefs could recite their ancestry back a thousand generations to their origins as descendants of the gods. David also had vast knowledge of the uses of the medicinal plants. David knew the exact places on the mountain where the plants were to be found. Some years later this medical knowledge was recorded on tape for the little museum we started in Wailuku, the county seat. David thought that his ancestors came originally from the Mediterranean region because in their history is the story of a big flood, which he related to the biblical story. He took us up on the mountain to show us where some of the rare plants grow and also to a place where his family owned some land. This is one place to which I return in my memory. Walking through waist-high ferns I am reminded of the fascinating history of the Hawaiian people.

Hawaiian civil society was carefully constructed; the laws and rituals rigorously enforced. The high chief, who owned the land, divided it into pie-shaped segments from the sea to the mountains and parceled it out to his people. This way a person could be self-sufficient, having access to the sea for fishing, arable land for farming and mountain forest for hunting.

From ancient times the Hawaiian people were accustomed to the hard work of wresting a living from the earth. With no metals in the volcanic rocks, they used only stone tools fashioned from the hardest basalt, such as that found at the top of 14,000 ft. Mauna Kea. Nets for fishing were made from coconut fiber or the rarer olona plant found high in the mountains. Besides the few plants and animals the first Hawaiians could bring from the Marquesas and Tahiti in their voyaging canoes, there were some indigenous plants from seeds brought by migrating birds. They wasted nothing, using seashells for scraping, bowls made of coconut shells for eating, leaves of the hala tree for weaving mats and baskets, fabric made of the beaten inner bark of a certain kind of mulberry tree, wooden bowls for storage, fishhooks carved out of bone and medicines for all kinds of illness and injury from plants. All of these were very labor intensive processes.

A deeply spiritual people, the Hawaiians believed that gods were in charge of every aspect of their lives. The high chiefs and chiefesses were thought to be descendants of these gods. Each could present his credentials by reciting this ancestry. With no written language, their history was recorded in chants and dances. The present-day tourist would be surprised at the slow grace of many of the ancient hulas, with the movements describing the meaning of the chants. The dances were done by both men and women, depending on the type of story being told. David Kahoʻokele's gentle wisdom gave us a feeling of closeness to these fine people, and we respected their traditions.

Because of the way that lava flows down a mountainside, caves are common. Small caves were used as burial sites for bones and often contained prized possessions of the dead. The bones were thought to contain the "*mana*" (spirit, strength) and were therefore carefully preserved and protected. This makes perfectly good sense. The body has no strength without bones. In our wanderings about the mountain we found such a cave containing human bones. We only looked in, knowing that it would be very unfeeling and disrespectful to enter, and especially wrong to touch anything.

Hawaiians, like Native Americans, are nature people. Their belief is that everything in nature is connected, part of a whole. They talked to the plants, to the rocks, to the water, asking permission for their use and expressing gratitude for the life they gave. And everything was done with prayers of petition and thanksgiving. The spirit world was everywhere. The people (*kanaka maoli*—genuine human beings) were all *ohana* (family). All were part of the *ʻaina* (the land), and everything had life. They understood very well that they had to live with what they had, and they kept the whole picture in mind, being careful not to destroy any part. Life was not easy, but it was good.

The Hawaiian word for breath is *ha*, and breath was life. The first Caucasian explorers and whalers to visit Hawaii found a well developed culture and complex social structure. They found the welcoming spirit of Aloha very much to their liking and took every advantage of the generosity of the Hawaiians. In return they brought alcohol, firearms and all of our "civilized" diseases to which the Hawaiians had no immunity and which decimated the population in a few decades.

When the missionaries arrived they found a rather chaotic culture in transition because of the influence of the whalers. The Hawaiians readily accepted Christianity, but the missionaries did not entirely understand the deep spirituality of the people and their total reverence for all of nature, and they needed to broaden the concept past the ha to include a Creator. So the Hawaiians, also unable to understand, called the missionaries *haole*, which can be translated "without breath" but is normally translated as "stranger" or "foreigner". Since Caucasians were the first strangers to arrive, all Caucasians are called "haole". The well-meaning missionaries took away some important features of the culture, such as their way of remembering history in the songs and dances of the hula. But they brought important features of Western civilization which the Hawaiians needed to cope with their changing world. Besides their very foreign and strict moral code, the missionaries gave them a written language, schools for their education, modern medicine to deal with the strange new diseases and counsel in their government. Hawaiians were eager students, and literacy was actually the highest in the world! Every Hawaiian child went to school.

The banning of the hula was over-zealous and unfortunate. With no written language, the hula was the literature of the Hawaiians. It told their stories in the songs and descriptive movements of the hula. The hula was their history, their poetry, their myths, their love stories, their jokes. After some years King Kalakaua had the ban removed, but many of the ancient stories had been lost or hardly remembered. Hawaiian history included stories of the large sailing canoes in which Polynesians had crisscrossed the Pacific many times and many centuries before Europeans dared to explore the Atlantic. They actually mapped the vast Pacific Ocean and knew where they were going, navigating by knowledge of the winds and stars and ocean currents.

As an infant in Alaska I was given a Haida Indian name. Mae Wallace, the wife of a famous carver of totem poles, gave me her own name, *Jahtsingaa*, which has a deep spiritual meaning. Since my mother could not give me a translation of my name, I had always wondered about it. On a trip up the Inside Passage to Alaska I found a Haida woodcarver by the name of Charles Natkong working in the Sheldon Jackson Museum in Sitka called his mother in Hydaburg and found my answer. It is Haida spirituality, and cannot be translated. I have never had any way of knowing how much this has affected my way of looking at the world, but I have the feeling that the influence may have been considerable. Add to this all that I received from my father, who grew up very close to nature in the hills of western Pennsylvania. Some of my happiest childhood memories are of nature walks with him. Because of Jim's Hawaiian name, I believe the same thing is true of his world-view. Living in East Maui in a remote and isolated area where the spirit of old Hawaii was still alive was a very special privilege, and every memory of our relationship with the mountain is precious. The mountain, born of fire and providing abundant amounts of water for the production of luxuriant tropical growth, expressed the extravagant generosity of creation.

• • •

The E.M.I. workmen sometimes went up into the forest to hunt the *pua'a* (wild pigs) which provided pork for their tables. After one successful hunting trip one of them brought us a piece of the choicest tenderloin, which I baked in my speckled blue enamel roasting pan. The flavor of the meat depends on what

the pigs choose to eat. I believe that some of the wild ferns give a
very strong taste and I suppose the country people had acquired a
taste for gamy meat. It was very much too strong for us. We
could not eat it at all, much to our disappointment. Nor could I
ever get the flavor out of the roasting pan, though I cleaned it
every stringent way I could think of. Never could I use that pan
again and finally had to discard it.

It was great fun to take our rare mainland visitors to enjoy
the wonders of East Maui. One adventure included traveling down
the "terrible" Hana road with the magnificent scenery, up a tiny
road to a locked gate, on up into Puohokamoa Canyon to a spot
where there was a spectacular waterfall. The sheer wall of the
canyon on one side was covered with blooming yellow ginger. In
the opposite wall was a water tunnel. On days when water from
this ditch was not needed on the plantation, the waterfall was
allowed to flow on down to the sea. When the water was needed,
it was diverted and ran into the tunnel. And the waterfall
disappeared! We loved to see the surprised look on the faces of
the guests as the waterfall suddenly stopped being there when
Richard turned it off and diverted it into the ditch tunnel.

In another canyon there was a hanging bridge across a deep,
narrow canyon, the only way to get from one side to the other.
Crossing a hanging bridge is a very strange experience. This one
was two or three planks wide with crosswise wires underneath
and a wire on each side to hold when negotiating the crossing. A
hanging bridge sways eerily as one walks, which gives a very
uncertain feeling. By the time the middle is reached there is a
very strong urge to go back to safety. With several following and
waiting for the experience, this does not seem to be an option, so
with great courage the rest of the crossing is somehow managed.

Part of a visitor's excursion would also include viewing the
Ke'anae Peninsula from the high, sheer cliff above. The peninsula
had many rectangular patches of *taro*, a staple of the Hawaiian
traditional diet. Taro leaves were the main green vegetable, often
cooked with coconut milk, and also used to wrap fish or pork
for cooking in the "imu" with hot rocks for the heat. The root

was pounded to make *poi*, which was the chief starch in the diet. After descent to sea level one could see that the fields of taro were kept wet by a waterfall and stream which could not be seen from above. A small village near the rocky coast contained an ancient church which was a very photogenic landmark with the black lava and blue sea as background. Before the war the Inter Island ships came to the Ke'anae peninsula. Small boats brought passengers and provisions to the edge of the rocky coast to be lifted manually by derrick and winch. The ships, the S.S. Wai'ale'ale, S.S. Mauna Kea, S.S Kilauea, and the Humu'ulu, which carried cattle as well as passengers, were taken into military service in 1942. Since that time there has been no regular surface travel between the Islands.

• • •

James Notley Thomas was born in the Pa'ia Hospital on July 17, 1946. For the first months of his life, our infant son went on the Sunday trips with us, of course. As we discussed what kind of family structure we wanted for his development, we agreed that Christian teaching was essential. To my husband that meant the liturgy of the Episcopal Book of Common Prayer. He had grown up with this, though he had departed from The Way for a long period of time. The nearest Episcopal Church was twenty-five or thirty miles around the mountain and across the valley. But, having made up our minds, the Sunday trip was in to the church, and the nature excursions were on Saturday. On April 5, 1947, our son was baptized James Notley Keli'iokamalu (the Hawaiian name given to him by the Rev. Daisy Kala'upa, the minister of the local church, the Kaulanapueo Huelo Church). And I was confirmed in the Episcopal Church by Bishop Harry S. Kennedy at the Church of the Good Shepherd in Wailuku, Maui.

During my pregnancy I had continued with daily walks, up into the forest behind our house usually wearing the green "fatigues" that an army officer had purchased for me at Ft. Shafter.

They seemed to be fairly rainproof, so they were convenient to wear in that climate, though I tried to take my walks between the rain showers. I went into labor quite a bit early, two and a half months early in fact. This was quite scary since Richard was somewhere out on the mountain, and I had no way to reach him. Cell phones were a long time later. The Hana telephone operator to the rescue! Miraculously, my husband was at home in a very short time, to take me in to the hospital in Paʻia. I could never understand how the operator managed to find him. A few days in the hospital, and no baby, but I had to stay in bed until the scheduled "due date". The irrigation company manager and his wife were away on a trip to Scotland, so we were able to stay in their house in town until the proper delivery time.

While we were at the manager's house my brother, Elvon Howe, came to Maui. He was on his way to witness the Bikini Island atom bomb test for his paper, the *Denver Post*, so his visit was very brief. This was the second time he had been in the Islands. The first time, I saw him in Honolulu during the war when he was stationed as an Air Combat Intelligence Officer on a small carrier. At this time I found myself at a social disadvantage, being pretty much confined to my bed, so he didn't see much of our beautiful Island. Showing off Maui was our favorite thing to do, so this was a great disappointment to me.

Well, now, I hadn't really seen a baby since my little sister, Helen, was born, so I had a lot to learn. And since the murky condition of the water coming from the faucets made it impossible to clean bottles, I realized that breast-feeding was a necessity. There was no way to clean and sterilize formula bottles properly—they were glass bottles, of course. Those were days when nobody, but nobody, breast-fed their babies. So I had no help with this, and it isn't always easy to accomplish satisfactorily. The hospital was no help at all. The nurses were so accustomed to bottle-feeding the babies that they would bring me the baby and leave him for a time, then take him back to the nursery and pour formula down through a nipple with a large hole. I had trouble convincing him that he was supposed to work a little. I was not in a very strong condition, but after two weeks in the hospital, we took our baby home. Though I didn't even know how to fold a diaper (they were cloth, of course) things did work themselves out. He thrived and gained weight appropriately and gave us lots of joy. One small, note—as an infant Jim was routinely put to bed before we ate our dinner. Occasionally the butcher would send some good calf liver with the weekly meat order. It seemed that every time this was on the menu Jim would start to cry just when we sat down to eat. Liver does not like to wait to be eaten, but if we tried letting him cry the liver tasted very dry. I don't believe I remember ever cooking liver since.

I was fortunate to have the daughter of one of the Portuguese workers come every day to help me clean and do the laundry. She was a sweet girl but so shy that she refused to eat lunch with me. There was a rain barrel outside the kitchen door to catch rainwater for washing and rinsing clothes. The water from the ditch after a rain was too muddy and just wouldn't do. A separate building was provided for washing and hanging the laundry on rainy days, which meant nearly every day. Normally it did not matter how long it took for things to dry, but with baby things it was different. We could not always wait. During the month of December, when Jim was an infant, every diaper and gown and sheet and blanket was dried in front of the fireplace. That was the month it seemed to rain all day every day—twenty-five inches in all. Things hung in the wash house seemed to be more wet the next day. I burned a huge old tree in the fireplace that month and got little else accomplished except to turn sheets, blankets, pajamas and diapers this way and that for drying on a rack.

Our little boy was slow to walk. At fifteen months he was still moving very quickly, crab-fashion. One day I happened to be watching when he got to his feet, walked across the room and sat down. He didn't try it again for six weeks, but after that he almost never fell down. Apparently he thought it over thoroughly to figure how this new walking business worked. At this he succeeded very well!

Jim loved the little garden, especially the string beans that grew on the fence and the poha berries that grew nearby. He picked them every day or two, and I made poha jam, as well as strawberry-guava jelly in season. These were my Christmas presents to family on the mainland. Poha are ground cherries; the common guava is a round, yellow fruit about two inches in diameter. The strawberry-guava is much smaller, red and has a strawberry flavor.

At Christmastime we started an ornament collection which continues to this day. The first were some exquisite hand-blown glass ornaments which somehow found their way from Czechoslovakia to Maui after the war. However, we ordered foil ornaments from Sears to put on the tree as far up as Jim could reach so that the tree would not be "mustn't touch!'

•   •   •

An annual event at the Huelo Church was Daisy's "poi lunch", actually quite a *lu'au*. There was the traditional imu-cooked kalua pig, accompanied by sweet potatoes, lomi lomi salmon, *opihi* (small shell fish), *opae* (tiny fresh water shrimp both cooked and raw), octopus cooked in coconut cream, poi, of course, *haupia* (coconut pudding), *kulolo* (a taro and coconut pudding), *kukui nut* paste, yellow cake with coconut frosting, and always orange soda. The opae tickled going down.

I liked to go and watch the preparation of the kulolo. The ladies gathered at the church, bringing freshly dug taro roots, coconuts, and little stools with graters attached. (The taro plant was a staple in the Hawaiian diet. The root from which the poi was made provided the starch, and the cooked leaves were the main vegetable.) Some of the ladies peeled the taro, others hand-grated the coconut sitting astride the low stools with serrated metal scrapers attached. The ripe coconuts had to be husked, broken open, and the white meat scraped out. Some squeezed the grated coconut through cheesecloth to get the "cream". The taro root was boiled until soft, then mashed and mixed with the coconut cream. This was then cooked underground with hot rocks for heat. The result was a delicious, sweet, brown dessert. To this event Daisy invited the county dignitaries, and they came—even traveling the treacherous Hana Road!

We enjoyed having papaya for breakfast, and we were happy to have several very sweet "solo" papaya trees in our yard. Solo papaya did not require a male tree nearby to provide fertilization. There was a male tree, which had beautiful, fragrant, pendulous clusters of blossoms. On the bearing trees the blossoms are singular, appearing on the trunk. One day I went out to find the Filipino yardman beating on the male tree with a stick. When I asked what he was doing, he replied that if you beat the tree "sometimes you can make it come different." He wanted the male tree to bear fruit.

On one side of our yard was a bank covered with gardenias, which were a delight to me. One year when there was a celebration in Honolulu I learned from the Hawaiian women how to handle gardenias and keep them fresh. With their expertise and help from their gardens, I packed about five thousand blossoms, which the airline carried to add to their fragrant beauty to the festive celebration. (If gardenias are handled with wet hands they do not turn brown, being protected from the oil on the skin).

• • •

Occasionally there would be dry periods when the rainfall was not sufficient to supply the sugarcane fields. Since it was not possible to store water in the porous lava of the canyons, the irrigation company decided to drill for underground water which would be available for transport through the ditches. The mountain was searched, and a promising place for drilling was found three miles up the mountain near the Kuhiwa River. A permit to bring in explosives to "blow the bottom" was not forthcoming, so the heavy drilling equipment had to be taken to the drill site by truck. When they tried to take the equipment to the chosen place, they found that boggy land through which they had to pass would not support the trucks. Someone had the brilliant idea to make a road of tree fern stumps. Plants grow to tropical size here, and tree ferns grow to a height of twenty to thirty feet. Stumps were cut and laid side by side for a distance of several hundred feet. As the heavily loaded trucks drove over the road the tree ferns stumps sank down at the point of contact, but supported the weight temporarily as the truck continued on its way. An engineering triumph!

One of the fun things that my husband got to do was to design and build a small dam on a stream near our house. Working on airplanes before the war had not provided the opportunity to practice this kind of engineering, so he enjoyed studying the site, choosing the right place, and designing and building the dam, which was of course known as "Daddy's dam" after our son, Jim, was born.

My husband's greatest challenge was the complete and careful examination of the entire system of ditches and tunnels and flumes. The open ditches were relatively easy to keep clean. The tunnels and flumes were another story. It was necessary to maintain a downward grade from the farthest canyon to the reservoirs in the valley. Where possible, the ditch ran along the mountainside. The canyon walls were steep, and it was necessary to tunnel through to the next canyon. The longest of these tunnels was two miles long, through the solid lava. The tunnels had been dug by some of the earliest laborers who came from Japan and were about five feet tall. Saihei Okada was the name of the man most responsible for the successful tunneling. My six foot four husband found examining any of the tunnels difficult. Getting through the two-mile tunnel was excruciating. In places the tunnels contained water. Examining the round flume pipes was a daring feat requiring courage. I was particularly glad to see him come home at night during these times. Fortunately this exercise wasn't required very often.

Those were strange, but wonderful years. We learned resourcefulness and adaptability. We learned to love the magnificence of the mountain and to appreciate the exuberant, lavish extravagance of nature in this marvelous place. We were awed by the size of the giant old trees in the koa forest, the variety of ferns, of vines, of gingers, and of the torrential rains that carved the canyons and supplied the waterfalls and streams. I think back on those years with tenderness and gratitude.

After more than three years in that special part of Paradise, we moved to the big plantation in the central valley.

PLANTATION LIVING
1949-1962

When we moved from East Maui to the central valley of Maui to a position with the Hawaiian Commercial and Sugar Company (HC&S), the largest of the sugar plantations, we lived in Pu'unene, the mill village. The house was an old plantation house very near the mill offices and the large sugar mill. The main street of the town ran in front of it and an irrigation ditch was one boundary of the yard. The old garden was lovely, with large monkey pod trees hanging with huge philodendron vines and an area planted with several varieties of heliconia. A beautiful Poinciana regia tree made a show of color in one corner of the yard, and a profusion of gingers added their fragrance. There was a good avocado tree in the back yard. Post Office Box 66, Pu'unene, was our mailing address for the rest of the time we were in the Islands. We kept this address even after we built our house in Sprecklesville because we preferred to use the Hawaiian name.

• • •

In the early days, the first sugar plantations needed agents in

Honolulu to represent them in making purchases, arranging cargo
space and selling sugar. They turned to small merchant firms
which had developed primarily to trade with the whaling fleet
and the native Hawaiians. These firms became the "Big Five",
Alexander and Baldwin, C. Brewer and Company, American
Factors, Castle and Cooke and Theo. H. Davies. Sugar cane was
planted on all of the larger islands, and sugar was the chief
industry. The largest plantation, the Hawaiian Commercial and
Sugar Company, on Maui, had 35,000 acres planted at its peak
production.

HC&S cane fields covered most of the central valley. Small
camps where the workers lived were placed for proximity to the
fields. The workers in each camp were usually of one ethnic
group—there were camps of Japanese, of Filipino and of
Portuguese. Many of the Chinese laborers, who had also been
brought to the plantations as field workers, had worked and saved
their way to having their own small businesses and had become
an important part of the economy of the Islands.

Sugar cane was grown as a two-year crop. This was possible
because there was no cold winter to deal with, and the two-year
cane had much higher sugar content than the cane that is harvested
in one year in much of the world. Planting and harvesting went
on continuously, so, there would be no seasonal lay-offs of
workers. When it was harvest time the fields that were mature
were burned. This got rid of much trash, and saved much weight
that did not have to be hauled to the mill in enormous trucks
manufactured by the Tournahauler Company which carried forty
tons at each trip. These trucks had replaced smaller trucks, which
had replaced the old steam locomotives, which replaced the horse-
drawn wagons which had originally hauled the cane stalks from
the fields to the mill. Surprisingly, the sugar content of the stalks
of cane was not affected by the burning.

At the mill the stalks of cane were washed thoroughly, then
crushed to extract the sugar. The juice thus obtained was boiled
and "seeded" with crystallized sugar to make more crystallization
begin. Large centrifuges separated the sugar crystals from the

molasses. The crystallized "raw" sugar was taken by truck to
Kahului harbor, where it was loaded into the holds of ships
to be taken to the California & Hawaiian (C&H) refinery in
California. The molasses was also shipped in bulk. The dry,
fibrous residue, called bagasse, was sold for the manufacture
of panels of "Canec" for acoustical ceilings and insulation.
Hawai'i's sugar industry is still the most productive in the
world, and the innovations made in all aspects of the work
have been to the advantage of sugar growers and millers all
over the world. The refinery, located just north of San
Francisco, was in what had been the Starr Flour Mill. This is
where all the raw sugar from Hawaii was refined.

After the harvest, the fields were plowed and replanted. Small
joints of cane were laid in the furrows to provide the next crop.
This replanting was done by hand. First-growth cane was left to
"ratoon", or grow again. This second growth nearly equaled the
first in sugar content. Water came in irrigation ditches from East
Maui or from one of the reservoirs on the plantation which had
been fed by those ditches. The mature cane grew to be thirteen
or fourteen feet tall, so the scenery changed dramatically in each
location every two years when the cane was cut. A roadway running
in the midst of fourteen-foot-tall sugar cane did not allow for
much of a view. When a large field was burned and cut, the
sudden vista-view for miles in the distance was quite startling.
There was an ever-changing drama of raw earth, new growth,
mature cane and the awesome spectacle of fields on fire. When
the field was plowed and replanted there followed weeks and
weeks of blowing red dirt—all just part of the cycle.

The newly planted cane was the result of years of
development. In 1895 the Hawaiian Sugar Planters' Association,
a cooperative of all the plantations, opened an experiment station
on the Island of O'ahu, Here new varieties of cane were constantly
bred to keep abreast of the problems that arose. One of these
problems was to develop cane so tough that the rats wouldn't
find it very tasty. Continuing experiments combated plant
diseases and also aimed to develop plants with higher sugar

content. An entomology department aided in biological control of pests. This was sophisticated farming.

The sugar cane was grown in the valley because it needed lots of irrigation. Pineapple did not require so much water, so it grew above the level of the irrigation ditches. Above the pineapple, in the Kula area, wonderful vegetables grew in the rich volcanic soil. And still higher, Haleakala Ranch ran cattle up to the boundary of the national park atop the 10,000 foot mountain. The cowboys (*paniolo*) rode fine horses, part Arabian and part Quarter Horse. They were fast and could turn quickly. This also made them excellent polo ponies, and the paniolo had great polo games for recreation. In Haleakala National Park, near the summit, is an area where the silverswords grow. These are large yucca-like plants with bright silver leaves. After ten years' growth they put up a flower stalk several feet tall that has hundreds of blossoms. After this magnificent effort the plant dies. This was the only place in the world where these plants were to be found.

Sugar cane was the life-blood of the Islands, grown in the lower areas of each of the main islands. The different plantations were managed by one of the half-dozen Sugar Factors, with headquarters in Honolulu. In the early days when the laborers were brought from China, Japan, the Canary Islands or the Philippines there were the well-known company stores. Due to their isolation and the difficulty of travel, the laborers had to do all their buying in these stores. In the early days wages were paid in script, almost all of which went to pay bills at the store, leaving little chance for saving. This was no longer true when we were there, but there was a difference in the amount of "intelligent selfishness" in the treatment of laborers on different plantations. In a letter home written in 1942 when I was working in Honolulu for Dr. Nils P. Larsen, who had organized the plantation health system, I described the situation at HC&S. "The common laborer has work, food, shelter, education, recreational facilities such as a movie theater and well-equipped playground, hospitalization, children's clinic, planned diets to suit the taste and pocketbook, and old-age and infirmity protection—and all free." HC&S was the largest plantation. Many of the smaller ones did not have all these facilities, but each plantation had its own hospital or used the one in a nearby plantation. These hospitals were staffed by doctors who had been trained by Dr. Larsen at the Queen's Hospital.

There was nothing in the world to compare with the plantation health system. This was finally recognized, Dr. Larsen having been awarded the "Gold Headed Cane", the highest national honor for industrial medicine.

These were the days after the war when the movement to unionize was very strong all over the country. Whatever the situation, I suppose workers always feel underpaid and under-appreciated. There is no doubt that each individual would prefer to be his own boss. There were legitimate grievances among Island workers, so that the International Longshoremen and Warehousemen's Union (ILWU) was able to sign up many of the plantation workers. The dock workers here and on the West Coast were also unionized, until the unions were strong enough to tie up shipping by striking a few dock workers in either location. The chief union organizer was Jack Hall, a Communist Party member under the direction Harry Bridges, president of the West Coast ILWU.

The plantation workers were the largest group, so with every new union demand a strike could be threatened. This threatened the entire economy of the Islands. Sugar was the economy of Hawaii. A strike in an agricultural industry is not the same as a strike in the automobile industry, for example. In Detroit the workers can lay down their tools, go back weeks or months later and pick up the same tools and tighten the same bolts they left, regardless of the weather. In an agricultural industry this is not so. If a sugar crop was ruined it would be a year and a half to two years before another harvest could begin, instead of the continuous harvesting of a normal cycle.

There were a number of strikes. One strike in 1946 lasted for several months. I remember this time very well indeed. No sugar was shipped for processing, and nothing came from the mainland—no food or other supplies. We were completely isolated, since we were entirely dependent on shipping from the Mainland. The union would not even begin negotiations until everything was set for the strike. Threats of strikes meant that Hawaiian sugar workers became the highest paid agricultural workers in the world, but workers and management became active adversaries.

The main talking point of the union organizers was convincing the workers that the "paternalism" of the plantations was taking away their rights. At that time nothing was quite as bad as paternalism. A result of this was that the plantation doctors opened their own offices downtown, and the workers were free to pay for whatever they thought they needed. (Ironically, it appears that now the unions are all in favor of paternalism, this time from Washington. Health insurance, workers' compensation, social security—these are all the things the plantations had provided.)

Communism and communists have not been much thought of since the days of the Cold War, but in the 1940's they were quite an important element in our national life. They were masters of intrigue and deceit and covert operations. A little book by Ichiro Izuka, a worker who joined the Party at this time, and later found that his leaders actually cared not at all for the workers, but only for the domination of Communism in the world, described their manner of operation here. In the conclusion to his book, *The Truth About Communism in Hawaii*, he says, "I quit the Communist Party because it is not honest with the workers. It is not interested in the workers of Hawaii as human beings or as individuals. Nor is it interested in this community as a place in which to grow up and live. It is merely interested in Hawaii as a favorable battle ground in which to wage the class struggle and win converts to Communism. Its loyalty is not to Hawaii or to America but to the Soviet Union".

I had been well aware of Communism, and understood it, since doing a year-long study of the Soviet system for eighth grade Civics. As the years passed I never had to revise my opinion and understanding. It worked just the way I had seen it working in 1928. What happened here was that the Union Movement got stronger and stronger by signing up laborers and striking for ever higher wages. No other agricultural workers in the world even approached the wages of Hawaiian sugar workers. And as a matter of fact, these very high wages helped to hasten the demise of sugar in the Islands. There are only two or three active plantations remaining. This has meant a great loss of jobs, so that most educated young people have to leave and go to the mainland to find good jobs.

The population of the island of Maui at this time was about 35,000, mostly plantation workers. There was a small sugar plantation in far-away Hana and one around the West Maui Mountains in Lahaina. But Paia Plantation, Hawaiian Commercial and Sugar Company in the valley, Wailuku Sugar Company on the side of the West Maui Mountains and the pineapple plantation on the side of Haleakala were close enough together to be one community. The "haole" on these plantations formed one social group. Besides the haole from the sugar plantations, a few others from the large cattle ranch farther up on Haleakala were included in this social group. The small towns on the island provided the everyday support services for the plantations and the general population. The County Seat, Wailuku, was at the base of the West Maui Mountains. In the central valley, Kahului, the port town, also had the airport nearby. Lahaina, at the other end of the West Maui Mountains, was also a port town, and had been a favorite residence for kings of Hawaii. The plantation at Lahaina was the Pioneer Mill Company.

●　●　●

Our move to the plantation brought an entirely different lifestyle than anything I had ever known before. Our son, Jim, was almost three years old at the time. Four of us mothers who had sons the same age, and who had similar interests, met every Tuesday morning from ten to twelve so that the boys could play together, and we could pursue our interests. For several years we made Christmas ornaments, starting in January. When we went to a Christmas party each of us had an ornament to take and hang on the tree or to include with packages or cards. Sometimes we took the boys to the beach for a change. Our favorite beach was in Kihei, where the water was quiet and fairly shallow; still we constantly counted heads in the water. One day a shark fin surfaced only a few yards from the children. You can believe that there was sudden activity as we got them out of the water! It was not a very large shark, and somehow it had got across the reef which protected the area. This was the only such episode.

Anything that Jim transplanted seemed to grow. When the new Maui Memorial Hospital was built on the hill between Kahului and Wailuku there was a long drive from the main highway. Jim dug forty-nine monkey-pod seedlings from under our huge trees and put them in juice cans. The earth was rich and soft and easy to dig. The plantation nursery had monkey-pod trees in five gallon cans, which they did not need at the time. So they exchanged Jim's juice-canned seedlings for the well-started trees. These were planted along the drive. The mature trees now line the drive up to the hospital.

When he was five years old Jim went to kindergarten in Kahului. The teacher was a dear little blonde who spent her afternoons scrounging for materials for her teaching. One item of interest was a small guinea pig. For some time Jim had been wishing and praying for a sibling. When the school year finished, the teacher was returning to the mainland and needed to find a home for the guinea pig. Jim wanted it, so we took Suzy home with us. Jim built a neat cage for her, played with her in the grass every day and took total and loving care of her.

Eventually it occurred to me that this was the ideal time to arrange for something to "be a mother". Mr. Rodrigues in Kahului raised all the guinea pigs for use in hospital testing on all the islands. I called him and presented our problem. He said to bring Suzy there and leave her for about a week and she would certainly be pregnant. We did. Mr. Rodrigues put Suzy in a cage with a large breeding male, and took some time to explain to Jim that the males were larger than the females, and that was the only way you could tell the difference. We had been home only a short time when Mr. Rodrigues telephoned. "Mrs. Thomas", he said, "You know that pig you brought down here? I went to check on her, and the pigs were fighting. Your pig is a male. But I found another pig with exactly the same markings. She is too young, but with pigs that don't matter. Do you want me to breed her?" I said that would be good. When we went the next week to get Suzy I explained to Jim that she had been away quite a while and she might not recognize him. On the way home with Suzy Jim examined her carefully and quietly and then said, "This isn't Suzy. Suzy had a brown spot right here on her neck." I had thought that Mr. Rodrigues had done a fine job and found the perfect pig, and I insisted that of course it was Suzy—the only time I ever told my son a flat-out lie. Well, Suzy didn't "get fat". So I called Mr. Rodrigues again. He said she must really have been too young, and to bring her back and leave her for another week. We did, and Suzy "got fat" and had two little piglets.

Suzy became a mother at just about the time we learned that there was a baby for us in a Lutheran orphanage in Nuremberg, Germany. Because Jim had continued to pray for a little brother or sister we had searched the world, but with dwindling hope. At the time we were also very much involved with the construction of a new house at the beach. Things happen that way, and I met Jane Gabriele in New York at Thanksgiving time in 1953. A petite blonde, our little Gay girl, was a constant delight. She moved with such grace that I decided she must certainly be a ballerina. For her third birthday I made a pink tutu and tiny ballet slippers. In photographs she seems hardly to be touching the floor. Two little girls lived across the street from us, and when one of them had a birthday I made her a little tutu of a different colored net. I did this for each birthday party that year, and they all wore their tutus to the parties. Gabriele took hula lessons from the premiere *kumu hula* (hula teacher), Emma Sharp, and was a lovely little dancer.

• • •

When a new residential area was opened on the Sprecklesville beach near the country club, we found a good lot there, and in 1953 we built our dream house. Our address there was 201 Kealakai Place, after a neighbor, Bea Savage, and I named the streets. We built a small three-bedroom house of hollow tile manufactured on Maui. Our Hilo architect friend worked with us to accommodate our wishes, then made every detail perfect. There were no wasted spaces, to the satisfaction of the engineer in the family, it was carefully designed until every detail seemed perfect, and it was declared "the best small house on Maui". A twenty-five foot window wall in the living-dining room, with clerestory windows above, opened to a large lanai overlooking the rocky black lava beach. At the dining room end water flowed down a wall into a small pool. There were lots of built-ins for convenience and space-saving. Jim's room had a private entrance from the lanai. We moved in just before Christmas in 1953.

Landscaping was important in plans for our house. Jimmy Fujimoto, a local artist, offered a class in landscaping at just the opportune time, and ladies from all regions enrolled—those who lived at the beach, those who lived in the valley and some who lived on the mountain. So besides the expertise of the artist-teacher I had the expert advice of those who knew by experience what would grow where. One bit of advice I did not take was that I could not grow gardenias at the beach. I did anyway, and found that I could grow them there. I always wanted to have gardenias. The house was on high ground, with a scooped-out area on the beach side in which we planted beach naupaka, plumeria trees for flowers for making leis and a small area of sugar cane. Richard chose a number of varieties including red cane and old-style "eating cane" which had been grown before the newer varieties were made resistant to rats. Sugar cane from different eras made this a little spot of history.

The trade winds blow between the mountains and across the valley, so that windbreaks are usually an important part of landscape planning. The sand dune we were on was a few feet above Kealakai Street. I chose akulekule (ice plant, a succulent) for a ground cover. It needed little water, and could be started from small pieces of the plant. If the day had been very windy, the next morning most of the plants would have rolled down the bank and have to be replanted. It took quite a while to make that ground cover be effective. At the top of the bank I planted an ironwood hedge, which I myself maintained at the height of ten feet. This was quite a project.

Jimmy Fujimoto also had a painting class which I took. The dining room wall in our house was paneled in Philippine mahogany. I had gone to the art shows looking for the right picture for that wall, without finding it. So I boldly decided to try to paint one in the colors that pleased me. I borrowed a blooming monstera plant from Betty Burnett and starting with a sketch, transferred it a 30x40 inch canvas. A lot of oil paint went on before I liked it at all, but it didn't please me enough, so I didn't hang it for at least a year after we were in our house.

In the meantime, Dr. Larsen kept in touch with his plantation doctors. He came to Maui several times to visit them, and was our houseguest after we were in our new home. He had always shown me his artwork, and whenever we went to Honolulu I would see his latest work. So I got up my courage and showed him my painting. He studied it a bit, and then said that it needed a touch of red on the edge of the blossom. I followed his advice and outlined the edge of the blossom with a fine red line. It made all the difference, and I finally did hang it.

On one of his visits I took him around to Kahakuloa—not a very good road, but with marvelous scenery. Passing by it on his flight home he made sketches. The next time he came to visit he brought an oil painting on coconut fiber of the mountains and waterfalls we had seen. At some point he had decided to try watercolors. His first effort used a pair of Ming horses on a coffee table for models. He painted them in a strong blue-ten horses' heads in extreme activity. The effect was powerful, reminding me of his seemingly endless energy. I studied this painting every time I was in Honolulu. On one visit it came to me as a gift! I framed it with a matching blue mat. It is an attention-catching treasure.

●　●　●

Part of our family was a small dachshund, "Heidi", which was given to us by a friend because she was not compatible with her pet, "Lady". We walked Heidi on the beach every evening. Fishing floats and bottles of all kinds that washed ashore were broken on the rocks and tumbled in the waves until they were smooth. I especially liked the blues and greens and picked up well-worn pieces each evening, including some that were clear or amber. These have since been a focus of interest, displayed in a large bowl on a white coffee table.

Lady came to live with us a year or so after we got Heidi, when her owner was married and went to the Riviera on a month's honeymoon. This was a very touchy situation, which was resolved by Lady herself. We had polished concrete floors with a small rug under the coffee table in the living room. Delicate Lady danced on her little toes and slipped all over the floor. She made it to the rug and stayed there. We took her off to go outside and to eat. Meantime, Heidi established her superior position and when Lady finally ventured off the rug and learned to walk on the floor they got along very well. As it turned out, Lady lived with us for a year and a month. The honeymoon couple stayed on the Riviera, bought a villa and came back a year later to get their dogs, leaving our Heidi with us.

●　●　●

The Maui County Fair was a big annual event. Besides the usual rides and booths, this was the craft fair where we could buy the beautiful hand made wooden bowls and woven lauhala mats and coasters. Of course there was a flower show, and one year I even won a small prize for an arrangement.

One year a prize was offered for an advertising ditty, and I wrote one to the catchy tune of "The Railroad Runs Through the Middle of the House":

Everybody goes to the Maui County Fair
Everybody's friends are going to be there
Everybody waits for the Maui County Fair
And it's more fun all the time.

It was chosen, and played on the radio, and played constantly at the fair, until I was sorry that I had written it. When we had toured the country on an educational trip for the children we visited Niagara Falls. I was pleased with one picture taken and had the nerve to enter it in the photography contest with all those excellent Japanese photographers. Much to my shocked surprise it won first prize! Five year old Gabriele entered Lady in the dog show where the children brought their pets and won prizes for the longest tail, the droopiest ears, the most spots, etc. As the events varied from day to day it was necessary to go each day. Altogether it was a thoroughly delightful country fair.

Jim enjoyed constructing model airplanes and painting them meticulously. He had a set of small plastic blocks with which he built a model of our new home. He had always liked to make intricate designs with tinker toys. He developed an interest in the night sky, and when he was in the sixth grade we got him a J.W. Fecker 4 inch Newtonian "Celestar" telescope. There were no street lights where we lived, and the Hawaiian skies are so clear that the stars seem to be very close. Jim spent many an hour studying the sky and taking pictures of the moon. He entered the county science fair when in the eighth grade, with a working model of a spectroscope, and a spectrogram to show how it worked. It won a prize, so he got to take it to the state fair in Honolulu. On our trip to the Mainland in 1960 we visited the Lick Observatory in California, the Adler Planetarium in Chicago and the Harvard Observatory. Jim enjoyed V.I.P. treatment, and was taken into the forbidden places while the rest of us waited on the sidelines.

Tracking satellites from the top of Haleakala brought scientists to the Island. Among these was Dr. Grote Reber, who was one of the original designers of radio telescopes. He came several times on his way to visit Tasmania, because he said there was a hole in the ionosphere down there which made better viewing with his radio telescope. This was so many years before we heard about holes in the ionosphere exposing the ozone layer in the atmosphere. Dr. Reber was also interested in Jim's spotted pole beans growing in the back yard. Since plants grow counter-clockwise below the equator, he wondered if they could be made to grow that way up here, and whether it made any difference in the number of spots they would have. So Jim went out every morning and wound yesterday's growth counter-clockwise. And every day they turned back to clock-wise. I don't remember about the spots, but we had some very frustrated beans. Jim says the white beans with black spots became black beans with white spots.

The children attended the Kaunoa English Standard School, a public school in which only correct English could be spoken, not "Pidgin English". Pidgin is a simplified speech, a conglomerate of words and phrases from different languages, spoken here with a local inflection. The school was about a half mile from our house, so the children could walk to school. There was a school rule that children could wear shoes or come barefoot or wear flip-flops, but if shoes were worn they had to be kept on. Most children were used to being barefoot, and my children preferred that. Jim finally had to wear shoes whenever he had office duty when he was in the eighth grade.

May Day is Lei Day in Hawaii. Every school had a Maypole and elected a king and queen. Selected boys carried the royal standards, the kahili, and girls were selected to be in the court to represent each of the islands. Each island has its own representative color and flower. It was quite a colorful pageant, with lots of leis made of different flowers, and pretty aloha shirts and muʻumuʻu.

Named from south to north, the colors and plants representative of each Island are:

> Hawaii-red, for the lehua blossom.
> Maui-pink, for the lokelani (rose).
> Kahoʻolawe-grey, for hinahina (Spanish moss)
> Lanai-orange, for the kaunaʼoa (a beach vine).
> Molokai-green, for the leaves of the kukui tree.
> Oahu-yellow, for the royal ilima blossom.
> Kauai-purple, with the mokihana lei.
> Niʻihau—with leis of tiny sea shells.

• • •

One summer the children planned a backyard circus with the two boys across the street. Jim had a little hand-set printing press which printed on 3"x5" sheets. Flyers were printed to distribute about the neighborhood. There were trapeze acts and a magic show and other original performances. I made elegant satin capes decorated with sequins and provided juice and cookies. There was a charge for the show, and all $3.61 was donated to a charity cause. This great bit of philanthropy was written up in the paper, and years later a friend sent a clipping from *The Maui News* in which the story was reprinted in the 25 Years Ago column.

When Jim was about thirteen years old, several boys his age got little sailboats. The boats were El Toros, which were little eight-foot sailing dinghies. They were quite stable and easy to handle, and the boys enjoyed sailing them in Kahului Harbor. At the end of the summer, before school started again, they had a race for a trophy, and Jim won! He has enjoyed sailing ever since.

At berry picking season the family went up on the mountainside where there was a large patch of wild blackberries to pick for making pies and jam. The thimbleberries grew out in the rain forest area. When a friend and I went there to pick, they were not as abundant as when we lived out there, and we usually ate most of them on the long way home. We went as much for the trip as for the berries, anyway.

Every few years a "Kona storm" would bring snow to 10,000 ft. Haleakala. This was an exciting event, and people rushed up to see it. Often the local people didn't take time to realize how cold it would be, and would go up in their shorts and zori (flip-flops). It was great fun to play in the snow and to make a little snow man to ride down into the valley on the front bumper of the car. The snow never lasted very long on the mountain, but the snowballs in the freezer at home lasted quite well.

• • •

Social life on the Island followed a pattern. "Everyone" was invited to the parties, and social obligations had a way of piling up. Most of us had some help with household cleaning, but few had regular maids. So the best way to take care of social obligations was to have dinner parties, buffet style, for a dozen at a time. This was manageable alone. A favorite buffet menu was a curry made of chicken or shrimp with rice, and perhaps ten or so condiments to sprinkle on top. Always there were bananas and home-made mango chutney. (Everyone had a favorite recipe.) Other condiments might include: chopped cashews or peanuts, finely chopped celery, chopped raisins, chopped green onions, grated egg, grated coconut, chopped bacon, sliced mango and sliced papaya.

Eventually it was necessary to have a big party and include everyone. We had three such parties in the dozen years we were on the plantation. One was in the Pu'unene house. One was an open-house when we built our own home and had the architect and his wife come from Hilo. And one was when Richard's brother's family came from Chicago for a visit. To include "everyone" meant that seventy-five to a hundred and twenty-five people were invited.

Patsy was the cateress who took care of the big parties, and Harry was the bartender. Both were very good and very dependable. Since the parties involved the same people, Harry got to know everyone's choice of drink, whether it was bourbon, scotch or gin. Vodka was not yet a popular drink. By the time someone approached the bar Harry would have the correct drink ready. (The drinks were served in six ounce glasses.) Because of Hawaii's even climate and the low rainfall in the central valley of Maui, the big parties could be planned for outdoors. Besides our own, there were several memorable parties. One was at the Haleakala Ranch manager's home in Kula. The von Tempsky family had been there for many years and the house was full of family treasures.

One occasion at an ante-bellum Kula home celebrated the return of a niece to the Islands. The best of the Hawaiian "music boys" were brought from Honolulu to play for an evening of dancing. These were musicians whom the niece would remember from former days—the same musicians who played for the moonlight dances at the "House Without a Key" in Honolulu. We were seated in the rose garden at tables with pink striped chintz tablecloths and monogrammed linen napkins and sterling flatware. By comparison my twelve place settings of Lenox china and sterling Towle flatware seemed rather minimal. The main course was beef stew, which we served ourselves from a large tureen. Dancing was on the broad lanai which stretched across the front of the house. The music was wonderful.

Few households had full-time maids, but most of us had some household help. When we lived in Pu'unene the old plantation house had a building in the back yard that had been for maid's quarters. Our children were small, and we had a Filipino girl from one of the plantation worker's camps who lived there and went to high school. She helped with the cleaning and was a ready baby-sitter. After we moved to the beach, three or four of us had the same cleaning lady who came for two hours a week, on the same day.

•   •   •

As I have written before, Richard and I were married in April of

1945 and went to Maui after the war was over. Our good friends, the Hardens, were married in May of that year—a month after our wedding—and went to live in Hilo on the island of Hawaii a month after we went to Maui, and the oldest of their four daughters was born a month after our Jim. Our families got together for a week every summer while the children were growing up. HC&S plantation had a beach house in Makena at the end of the road on the Kihei side of the island. It was large and rambling and slept twelve comfortably. We asked for it for a week each summer. One year the Hilo family would come to join us there, and the next year we would go to the Big Island and join them at some beach site. The Makena beach was a wonderful place for our two children and their four girls to be together.

One of the older girls recalls a day when she built a raft of sorts and put very small Gabriele on it for a ride. She says that I became aware of the enterprise and quietly suggested that it might not be such a good idea. I have not the slightest recollection of the occasion, but she remembers it well.

Our little Gabriele liked to fish. Her father sometimes took her fishing in one of the plantation reservoirs, where she almost always caught some fish. I well remember one morning at Makena when she and the youngest of the four girls came quietly down the corridor at six o'clock to waken me and ask if they could go fishing in the tide pools. Tide pools are lovely at any time of day, but there is a very special quality about the world at dawn. They did catch one four-inch fish which they insisted should be cooked for breakfast.

The four girls are now scattered from Paris to Hawaii, but the children have maintained contact through the years.

•   •   •

When we went to Honolulu we referred to the trip as "going to town". This was always by air; there being no surface transportation since the inter-island ships were taken for service during the war. These trips were sometimes just family excursions or perhaps when Dick had business trips. We were told that Island residents could stay at the Royal Hawaiian Hotel for ten dollars a night. This sounded highly improbable, and the first time we tried it we saw the price on the door—seventy-two dollars. It was quite a relief to find that our bill was only ten dollars a night. Actually! A big treat for the children was to ride the city bus. School buses were the only transportation of that sort on Maui, and our children walked to school. The most special thing for Gabriele was to eat lunch at the Honolulu Woolworth's. Gay did not like restaurants because she couldn't be sure what she was ordering. The Maui Woolworth's did not have a lunch counter, but the Honolulu one did, and there were pictures on the wall in front of her. Choosing from the pictures was delicious.

When we sailed on a British ship for the Mainland in 1960 someone gave Gabriele a copy of Dr. Seuss's "Birthday Book" with pictures of a smorgasbord. She spent the entire trip hoping to see a place to eat where the food was presented as in the fanciful book. She did have one triumph, however, at the Empress Hotel in Victoria where she encountered her first cafeteria, with all the food right there before her to choose from. The choice was never difficult or time-consuming because she always chose the roast beef and mashed potatoes.

•   •   •

Once a year the members of top management from all the sugar plantations on all the islands met together at the Royal Hawaiian Hotel in Honolulu. The Royal was owned by the Matson Navigation Company, and the dinner menus used the same covers as first class ship passengers used. The covers were copies of John Kelly color etchings of Hawaiian themes, with a different one for each evening. Happily, one year I thought to bring ours home with us. Years later I had them framed, and we have enjoyed them ever since. Now they are quite valuable, as John Kelly has been "rediscovered". I had known John Kelly as Dr. Larsen's friend, and he gave me a print of his etching of an old man, "Old Kalama" for a wedding gift. It hangs on my wall beside another numbered print of "The Lone Fisherman".

Dick's job as head of the Department of Research and Development brought him into contact with sugar growers from South Africa and Australia as well as agriculturists from the University of California at Davis. When they came with their wives to see how things were done in the Islands, I spent my days showing the wives about Maui and/or having them to dinner. Since I had come to the Islands with the idea of being on my way around the world, I especially enjoyed meeting the people from distant places. We continued Christmastime correspondence with the couple from Natal, South Africa for several years. The Australian couple had visited Texas before coming to Maui. When we had them to dinner they told about seeing the bison. The name confused them, since with their Australian inflection a "bison" (basin) was something they used for washing their hands. This was a very amusing story, and they enjoyed laughing at themselves. When they returned home they sent us an Australian "bison", a signed porcelain bowl with a painting of an aboriginal man.

Several times a representative from the consulting firm of Arthur D. Little came for a consultation. During one visit the representative invited Richard and me to go to dinner at the Hotel Hana Maui. It would take too long to go by car, so he arranged for a plane to take us. This delighted me no end. Having traveled in and out of those magnificent gorges along the infamous Hana Road to East Maui so many times, the thought of seeing them from the air was quite thrilling. The idea was less than thrilling to Richard, who did not trust small planes in such country. Neither of us won. It so happened that one of the volcanoes on the Big Island of Hawaii was in furious eruption and the usually dependable trade winds were not blowing the smoke and ash away from the islands. There was a thick blanket all the way to Oahu. We did fly to Hana, much to Richard's discomfort and my disappointment. We flew very close to the water and could hardly see the edge of the land, let alone see up into the canyons. So much for my one small plane trip over Maui.

We did have a much more satisfying experience with a volcanic eruption. In 1952 the Kilauea volcano erupted for one hundred three days on the island of Hawaii. This eruption was neatly contained in Halemaʻumaʻu, the huge caldera which is called the "fire pit", and the home of the goddess Pele. Eruptions have occurred there from time to time through the centuries. As Island people are wont to do, we went to see it. At that time we could stand right at the edge of the cliff and watch the lava fountains below. A letter written home gives my account of it at the time:

"When we learned that Kilauea was active again for the first time in eighteen years, we joined the thousands who thronged to the 'Big Island' to watch the show. We saw it by night and by day as continuous fountains of molten red lava raised the floor of the fire-pit inch by inch.

"By night it was hypnotic. Pele, goddess of fire, who lives on the island of Hawaii now, brought some of her lava out of the earth. She threw it in fountains from 100 to 400 feet into the air, then let it fall again to cover the floor of the fire-pit with fresh "*pahoehoe*" (smooth lava) in great slow waves. Smoke, sulphur, pumice and the long, thin strands of "Pele's hair" were carried by the wind across Kilauea Crater and all along the side of the great mountain, Mauna Loa.

"The crater is approached from the port town of Hilo, about thirty miles away at the base of Mauna Loa. Hilo is the center of the thriving orchid industry in the Islands, and nearly every yard seems to have a few square feet to an acre of so of lavender vanda orchids growing in it. Outside of Hilo the highway is as beautiful as a garden path as it passes mile after mile through fragrant ginger, tree ferns, luxurious vines, and guava and other trees. As we climb higher, the vegetation

changes to lichen-covered 'ohi'a trees on bare lava.
The lava flows are recent enough that very little
soil has been formed.

"Kilauea is a smaller mountain on the side of
Mauna Loa (Long Mountain). The summit
caldera, is a crater two and one-half miles long
and two miles wide, at about 4,000 feet elevation.
The area of the floor of the crater is about 2,600
acres. 'Halema'uma'u', meaning the home of the
ma'uma'u fern, is the name of the big fire-pit in
the floor of the crater. Ten days ago the pit was
750 feet deep; two days ago it was 650 feet deep.

"As we drove up the mountain road we watched
the cloud of smoke rising from Halema'uma'u. It
was evening, and the pink glow from the eruption
blended into the sunset sky. As we approached
the rim of the fire-pit police directed us to safe
parking places. We then walked toward the noise
and the smoke. By this time it was dark, and as
we looked over the rim of Halema'uma'u at the
brilliant orange-yellow glowing fountains from the
earth's hot center, that spouted near the middle of
the pit, and at the undulating, undulating, boiling,
bubbling orange pools here and there we had a
feeling of unreality—almost of detachment. Pele
was there! Perhaps we had no right to be there!
Pele was in complete control—tossing her fiery
hair, dancing her wild dance to the drum-like
music of the rumbling earth and spreading her
lava with an indolent power as if to remind us
that she does not always sleep.

"We watched with fascination as fountains of
lava darkened from orange to red and then to gray,
even as they fell, then flowed slowly in black waves
veined with lines of red. The sound of escaping
gas was like the report of guns as it bounced off

the walls of the pit. The great cracks in the lava we were walking on kept us aware of frightening possibilities, for the earth quakes with the escape of the gasses and lava, and settles to fit its re-adjusted volume.

"Mauna Loa is the world's largest single mountain. It rises from 18,000 feet below sea level to 13,680 feet above—more than 31,000 feet. Its volume is nearly 10,000 cubic miles. As we drove up to the fire-pit the next morning we passed through the clouds and had a wonderful view of the tremendous and majestic mountain. The contour is a smooth curve, which tends to minimize its size in perspective.

"Black and white koae birds were dipping and swooping around the crater and the fire-pit, their white tails catching the sun. Occasionally one would dip too far, be caught into a down-draft and lost in the molten lava. We were told that these tropical birds belong to Madame Pele. If she wants them in her lava it is her own affair.

"By day the movement and activity on the whole floor of the fire-pit was easier to see. The lava fountains were red against the black waves moving away from them. A little cinder cone that was being built up at one end of the pit was sending out intermittent puffs of smoke. The bubbling pools at the other end of the pit were much more active than they had been the night before. And the whole sight seemed somehow more believable in the daytime. We knew that we were standing on a mountain, not simply on the edge of a fiery chasm. However, it was no less impressive as we watched the ever-changing patterns of the lava fountains and flows.

"As we left the crater by the road along the

rim opposite Uwekahuna, we watched as the
vegetation changed from small, scrub ohiʻa and
pukeawa (which resembles juniper) and sparse
grass to large, wizened-looking ohiʻa trees, giant
tree ferns, ginger, ti and colorful wild flowers, we
sat a few minutes on the lanai of the Volcano House
Hotel, looking out across Kilauea Crater toward
the smoking pit of Halemaʻumaʻu, before starting
down the mountain into the clouds below."

• • •

Most of the time life on the plantation was routine and
every-day. Work days began early, the men went home to
lunch, and we sometimes had meetings or a concert at night
but an occasional day is sharply remembered, as the day I could
not find Jim. We were living in the old plantation house in
Puʻunene, located at an intersection of the main street. One
side of the yard was bordered by an open irrigation ditch,
which was covered part of the way to the dairy a mile or two
away. Jim was a very dependable child, and I did not have to
worry too much about his going out into the street or too
near the irrigation ditch or out of the yard, though I did keep
careful watch. On this morning he was not in sight and did
not answer my call as I went all about the yard. No Jim. He
was not in the street. The ditch was the only other place, and
he was not in sight there either. Frantically I called his father
to alert the dairy workers to watch for him to appear in the
ditch. I kept calling, and finally he did appear—from the
neighbor's yard. There was a lot of growth between our houses,
and the wind had blown my voice away so that he could not
hear me calling. He had chased butterflies from our yard to
theirs. Time seemed to stand still as I waited for a call from
the dairy, when Jim would appear in the current in the ditch.
I was weak with relief when he came from the neighbor's yard
right next door. I can still see the look of puzzled surprise on

his face when he appeared, quite contented and happy, but suddenly startled at my emotional greeting. These are moments one never forgets.

·   ·   ·

As with any small community, responsible people did their part to make things work. Richard took his responsibility seriously in civic life and in his faith community. He was a member of the Rotary Club. For one or two years he headed the United Fund drive. He was a Boy Scout leader. He taught Sunday School in Good Shepherd Episcopal Church in Wailuku. He was a vestryman there and several times was Senior Warden.

One year when he was Senior Warden the parish was looking for a new rector. He happened to be making a trip to Honolulu at the time and was given the task of interviewing a prospective rector. He went with a page or two of a check list of things he thought important. The man being interviewed was Claude DuTeil, who later started a "peanut ministry" for street people in Honolulu which has grown to be an important out-reach and welfare ministry to homeless men and families. When Dick took out his check list for the interview, Claude laughed and said that he had not seen that before. He did appreciate it, however, since he was a graduate of Georgia Tech in Atlanta, and a check list is just the way an engineer would approach the matter. Ever the engineer, Dick might say, for example, "That measures approximately eleven and seven-eighths inches."

My civic activities included teaching Sunday School, P.T.A., helping to start the little museum, *Hale Ho'ike'ike* (Place of Display), which is now the Maui County Memorial Museum, and being on the board of the Maui Philharmonic Society. The best musicians of the day, who traveled the world, came through Honolulu and were contracted to play with the Honolulu Symphony. Every year we contracted with a half dozen to come and play for us. This contract included an afternoon concert for school children as well as the evening concert. Many, if not most, had never played to children and were somewhat apprehensive. They were always well rewarded. Children were bussed from all the elementary schools to fill the 1200 seat auditorium. If they dared to make any noise or misbehave in any way, they knew that they would be unceremoniously removed and never permitted to get out of school for an afternoon again. They never did. In their years of school they got quite a taste of classical music. Surely it has made a difference in their lives. The last concert of the year was always a group from the Honolulu Symphony and sometimes the entire symphony. They demonstrated individual instruments for the children. Surely this introduction to classical music has added something to the children's lives.

One year I served as Arbor Day chairman for the Maui County schools, which included the islands of Molokai and Lanai. This proved to be a very good learning experience for me as I researched the right variety of trees for the various climates. The children learned appreciation for nature as they participated in the planting of trees. Some schools were located near the ocean beaches; some were well up the mountainsides. Some were where it was very wet, others in extremely dry areas. To thrive, the trees had to be selected that were appropriate for the location. Ever since then I have been quite aware of the differences in the types of trees in other places we have lived.

•   •   •

Richard remained in the Naval Reserve after the war. There was no active Navy unit on Maui, but he became the local representative of the admiral in command of the Pacific fleet. There was no remuneration for this other than adding "brownie points" which eventually meant that he retired with the rank of Commander in 1960. This was a duty he enjoyed. It involved making docking arrangements for all ships coming to Maui and meeting the ships to take care of any special requests. He also liked to entertain the skippers and executive officers. I cooked for French, Canadian, Peruvian, Italian and Japanese, as well as the American ships, and it was interesting to meet all the officers.

In return for these favors the skippers would give us special tours of their ships. Sometimes they would invite us to lunch. At one lunch on an American submarine, baked Alaska was served as dessert. Ward room space on a submarine is very small, and it was quite a hot day. I was sure that the baked Alaska would slide off the large platter onto someone before they had served it all around the table. Fortunately there was no disaster. One Monday morning we had pink champagne on a French ship. And I remember the skipper of a Japanese ship leading us through a passageway calling "*dozo, dozo*" (please, follow me). The entire Japanese community celebrated when the Japanese four-masted training ship sailed into Kahului. I learned a short welcoming speech in Japanese for the evening banquet. The Tokyo-born wife of the Buddhist priest in the town of Paia helped me with this, and it was a great surprise to the local Japanese.

Once three Japanese frigates were in port at the same time. Besides the skippers and their executive officers whom we invited to dinner, we asked Stephen Okada and his wife. Stephen was a young Japanese engineer who worked in my husband's department and the son of Saihei Okada who dug the tunnels in East Maui. The Okadas demurred and tried to refuse our invitation. They insisted that they were not of an appropriate class to socialize with the Japanese officers. Stephen was concerned that the officers would recognize this. The Okadas' parents came from poor peasant families who had left their homes to travel thousands of miles in order to make some kind of living. They had worked hard and saved their money to send their son to college. Stephen was a graduate engineer and very intelligent. Dick insisted that the Okadas must come, to show how things are in America. It was a very successful evening, and I think we got the message across. These captains brought gifts—one gave us a beautifully framed print, the other two each gave me a Mikimoto pearl. These I had made into earrings.

Another story is a comment on Japanese culture. A Japanese

man who worked in Dick's department had been crippled since a childhood car accident. He lived with his mother, who cared for him with the special attention given to boys. Approaching middle age, he considered that his mother would not be around forever, but he would still need help. We had heard of Japanese picture brides. In fact, many of the single men who came in the first groups of laborers exchanged pictures with Japanese girls and arranged for marriages with them. This man did something similar. He made contact with relatives in Japan to search for a suitable bride for him. He thought that an American Japanese girl would not be willing to wait on him the way he was accustomed to being treated. He found the perfect candidate—a young widow with three daughters. She would have no possible prospect for any kind of life in Japan. So he went to Japan and brought her back to the Islands. The marriage seemed to work ideally, and they later had a son. We enjoyed a very traditional Japanese meal in their home.

Three ships of the Royal Canadian Navy came several times, anchoring in Ma'alaea Bay for several days each time. They became known in the community. The officers were quite charming, and the community responded with a festive feeling. They were invited into other homes, and there were parties aboard their ships. On their last visit, their Maui friends wanted a party all together. So one was planned at our house, although I thought it was someone else's turn to host this one. The officers were entertained in various homes during the day and came to our home in the evening. It rained that day, and the wind came up. By evening it was a real storm, but everyone came. When the front door was opened the rain blew all the way across the living room. We had counted on using the low garden for party space, but everyone had to be packed into the living room and lanai. Later we found out that the storm was actually a hurricane, which meant that the wind was blowing at least seventy-five miles an hour. I was very sorry that the party was at our house because the living room was a swamp, and it took weeks to get the polished concrete floor back in condition.

• • •

This next paragraph shall be titled "How we did not get to meet Leonard Bernstein." In 1960 we took a three month, 11,000 mile trip across the mainland. The children were old enough to benefit from the experience. At the end of the tour we were house guests of the treasurer of the Portland Symphony, and Leonard Bernstein was conducting a concert while we were there. The concert hall was quite a distance from High Point, where we were staying, and we got into a terrible traffic jam on the way. After sitting for an hour and a half on the road, we returned home in disappointment. As fates would have it, it so happened that Mr. Bernstein was to celebrate his fiftieth birthday on Maui, and a big lu'au was being prepared. Since I was a board member of the Maui Philharmonic Society we would have been invited. However, our return trip on a British ship sailed from Vancouver, arriving into Honolulu harbor the day after the birthday party. And that is how we did not get to meet Leonard Bernstein.

Later a special person from New York came to be on Maui for a time. The Rev. Dr. Shelton Hale Bishop was the retired rector of the largest Episcopal congregation in the U.S., located in Harlem. He retired in the Islands, where the spirit of Aloha blurred the distinctions between skin colors. He was very light colored and blue-eyed but regarded as "black" by definition. There was really not much obvious racial tension in the Islands at that time. But I suppose we were living in our own privileged world and probably not paying much attention. As with any society, there is class consciousness and class envy. There were very few African-Americans in the Islands, however. When we became aware that this marvelous gentleman was not quite "accepted", I guess this shocked me. We preferred to give him the respect he was due, and he apparently recognized the difference. When we left the Islands in 1962 Dr. Bishop arrived at the ship with a dozen yellow roses for me. I have a copy of his little book "The Wonder of Prayer", which is a gem of spirituality.

Another of Dr. Larsen's good friends, David Kahanamoku, came with his blonde wife, Helen, to live on Maui. He was the brother of the famous "Mayor of Waikiki", one of five brothers, four of whom were winning swimmers in four consecutive Olympic Games. This was the David who was chosen as the perfect Polynesian to be represented in the Hall of Man in the Field Museum in Chicago. At the age of sixty-five, David had the physical condition of a man half his age. Each of the few Hawaiians I had the privilege of knowing at all well had an intangible quality of spirit to which I responded with veneration. David Kahanamoku had this quality. David Kahoʻokele, our good friend in the Ditch Country, had this quality. Mary Kawena Pukui, the authority on Hawaii, also had it. There was a certain dignity and assurance which I believe was part of their heritage of awareness of the sacredness of life and of nature. I was very much honored when David gave me a pen and ink portrait of himself at the age of thirty-nine, which had been made by a young naval officer. Richard's daughter, Starr Klube now treasures it.

Because of Richard's naval responsibilities we got to know Lt. "Kirk" Kirkpatrick who was in charge of the Coast Guard cutter stationed on Maui. He had seen duty in the Antarctic. While there, he had visited New Zealand, where he met red-headed Liz, the daughter of the Minister of Agriculture, and they were married—a very attractive young couple. When they came to Christmas dinner with us Liz asked to bring an English plum pudding, which was quite a hit. From then on we had plum pudding at Christmas. The attraction turned out to be that the puddings were full of dimes. But when dimes became sandwiched with copper and could no longer be baked into cakes, plum puddings went out of favor. We were asked to dinner with the Kirkpatricks when Liz's father sent a quarter of a New Zealand spring lamb. This proved to be just enough for the four of us for one meal, and I haven't tasted anything like it before or since.

While the Kirkpatricks were stationed on Maui, a very strong earthquake in Chile caused a tsunami which was expected to reach the Islands in force. Remembering that tsunami from Alaskan earthquakes hit our side of the island, we assumed that one from Chile would hit the other side. The Kirkpatricks lived on the beach on the other side so we invited them to come to our house. This wave arrived at night. We were surprised by the noise of the water. It was a dark night and we could not see the water from our higher spot. In the morning we discovered that the wave had come right up to our low garden. And much to our surprise there had been very little wave action on the other side of the island!

A curiously historic event happened when a neighbor across the street from us at the beach built a boat which they sailed in Ma'alaea Bay, where the humpback whales come to breed. They were sailing one day the neighbor's wife went below for a nap. She was awakened by a strange singing sound, which we decided must have been made by whales. For years and years I watched for reports of whale songs, and it is only in recent years that they have been documented.

My memory does not bring to mind which visitors wanted to go to the top of Haleakala for the sunrise, but that was a most memorable experience! Arising at 3:30 a.m. we set forth. It is a long, winding road to the summit, but we were there before the sun was over the horizon. It was a beautiful, clear morning, and we could see the Island of Hawaii in the far distance. The morning light on the cinder cones in the crater cast shadows, and the colors seemed deeper. After the sun had been up for a short time thin clouds surrounded us, and we made angel-like reflections of ourselves in the clouds (Brockenspecters), which appeared directly before us. Coming down the mountain into the bright valley we were sure we had been in another world. I always thought we would do that again.

•   •   •

In 1955 Dick was sent to Lake Placid to a three-month seminar on Industrial Engineering, which was a new approach to understanding work habits. The instructor was Dr. Lillian

Gilbreth. She was the widow of Frank Gilbreth, who was the pioneer of time and motion studies to determine the most efficient way to accomplish a task. Lillian Gilbreth was the mother in the book, "Cheaper by the Dozen". Mrs. Gilbreth wrote the story of her husband's life—"The Quest of The One Best Way". Frank Gilbreth died, leaving her with the twelve children and his unfinished dream of spreading his new gospel of work simplification. Mrs. Gilbreth valiantly assumed full responsibility, and became in demand world-wide as a teacher and lecturer. Richard Thomas was greatly impressed by the course at Lake Placid, and when she was on her way to lecture in Australia a year or two later, he arranged for her to speak to the Hawaiian Sugar Planters. She was about the age of eighty when she came to Honolulu. We went to Honolulu for this meeting, to hear Dr. Gilbreth speak. I was quite as charmed as Richard and had a conversation with her when he introduced us. Imagine my awed surprise when she invited me to inspect the new Tripler General Army Hospital with her the next morning. I went along, feeling rather like a fifth wheel. This wonderful visit began a correspondence between us.

A year or two later Dr. Gilbreth had another trip "Down Under", and we invited her to come to Maui on the way. This she did and spent two or three days with us. I thought it would be fun to invite ladies her age to lunch—there were eight or ten, and each one was quite sure that she was the oldest one present. Actually the oldest was eighty-four, as I recall. Dr. Gilbreth lived in New Jersey and continued her travels and teaching to the age of eighty-nine. Later, when Richard was with the Boeing Company in Huntsville, Alabama, working on the Apollo 10 program, Dr. Gilbreth came to speak to the NASA engineers. This was her last speech before final retirement—and we were there!

Our favorite neighbors across the street on Kealakai Place were Mary Jane and Alex McBarnet. Mary Jane grew up in Honolulu, and went to India after college. There she met Alexander J.W. McBarnet, an Englishman who had been born in

Southern Rhodesia, and had flown fighter planes with the R.A.F. Amazingly, he had survived the battle of North Africa, the Battle of Britain and the war in Europe. He never would show me his medals. Mary Jane and I improved our suntans, lying in the grass in the Hawaiian sun after lunch on many a day.

•   •   •

Best of all were the visits from family. The only brief visit from my brother, Elvon was actually while we were still living in the country and he was sent to witness the Bikini atom bomb test. I had seen him just once during the war when he came through Pearl Harbor as Air Combat Intelligence Officer on a small carrier, on his way to the far Pacific.

In 1954 we had just moved into our new home at the beach when my sister Dorothy and Dr. George Powers came through on their way to Guam. George had a naval internship, but the war was over before he had finished his required three years of service so he was called back during the Korean War. Theirs was just an over-night visit, but I had not seen my sister since her college graduation.

In 1959 Richard's daughter, Lynne Starr, came to visit for the summer. She had just finished a year of college at the University of California in Santa Barbara. A beautiful young girl, she had a very busy social summer, and especially enjoyed the week at Makena beach in the plantation vacation cottage. She went off to Berkeley to college in the fall. In 1961, after seven and a half months touring Europe on a shoestring with her dear friend, Judy, and two and a half years of college, Starr came to live with us on Maui. That summer she did the usual home-from school student thing and worked in the Maui Pine pineapple canning factory. The next school year she attended the University of Hawaii in Honolulu.

Also In 1959 the Starr Thomas family came from Chicago for a visit—Starr, Virginia, Julie and Katie. They were here long enough for us to have one of our big parties and show them the island from Hana to Lahaina. With daughter Starr here we were the entire Thomas family all together. Our celebration of Julie's eighteenth birthday was a memorable occasion. We arranged for a picnic on the beach at Ka'anapali. This was private Pioneer Mill property, and we were the only ones on the beach—the same beach that now has ten beautiful resort hotels on it.

On our trip to the rain forest and Hana we had a bit of a scare. After taking our turns at negotiating the hanging bridge we found our way up a tiny road and walked to a small, enclosed area, stepping across a little stream on the way in. There was a lovely little waterfall feeding the stream. Richard was just telling us that if there were sudden rainfall higher up the waterfall could just as suddenly become a cascade which the stream couldn't handle and there would be no way out. At about that moment the waterfall began to be a torrent. We were barely able to get back across the little stream to safety!

We seem to have managed a lot of activity during this visit. Our Haleakala trip included hiking through the crater. From the end of the road at the summit is the "Sliding Sands Trail" which descends to the floor of the crater. A path then crosses the crater to a steep ascent on the other side. A switch-back trail goes up the nearly vertical side, ending very near the silverswords. Richard, brother Starr, daughter Starr, Julie, Katie and Jim made this trip. Virginia and I and five-year-old Gabriele came a little way down the switch-backs to wait for them. Waiting was very long for the small one, and she kept wanting to go just a bit farther down the trail that we would have to climb again. When the very weary hikers finally arrived we started on up to the top. At the 10,000 ft. elevation climbing takes energy. Every little while Gabriele would say, "Can't we just sit down and rest for a minute?" I would reply that we were getting close to the end, where the car was waiting for us. I held her hand and just kept tugging her along. The men were much too tired to consider trying to carry her, so there was a completely exhausted mother and child by the time we finally made it up to the road.

My sister Helen's visit came in 1960, and we had a great time sight-seeing. Included was one of our summer weeks at the Makena beach house. One day we went on out to LaPerouse Bay where the Hawaiians made their salt in "salt pans." These were shallow hollowed-out lava basins in which the Hawaiians evaporated sea water to make salt. Of course we showed her the "Ditch Country", and she saw the waterfall turned on and off. She saw the spectacular view of the Ke'anae Peninsula from the cliff above. We went on past Hana to picnic at the Seven Sacred Pools.

We also went to historic Lahaina, stopping along the way at the beach at Olowalu to find "Hawaiian diamonds". From one of the mountain streams—no one knew which one—very hard, clear stones washed down to the sea. They were encased in black lava which was gradually eroded away as the rocks were rubbed back and forth in the sand. Some of them washed up on the beach at Olowalu. It was fun to find them. They were harder than sapphires, and some of them were clear enough to look like diamonds when cut. In historic old Lahaina we walked under the enormous banyan tree, visited the old hotel, saw some of the original missionary houses and the old jail. We went on up to Lahainaluna School along the avenue of Royal Palms. This school, started by the missionaries, has the first printing press west of the Mississippi River. It was used to print in the Hawaiian language, and is now in a museum in Honolulu. Because of the work of the missionaries, Hawaii at that time had the highest level of literacy in the country. Lahainaluna School was situated above the town of Lahaina, overlooking the bay.

In 1962 the ownership of the plantation changed, and all the management changed, too. Again we left by ship for the mainland, to go to New Orleans for the Boeing Company, which was helping with the construction of the "Apollo" spacecraft and had offices in New Orleans and Huntsville, Alabama.

THE WAY IT IS
2002

Almost sixty-five years later Honolulu hardly seems like the same place. When we moved to Maui and "went to town" once or twice a year, we began to see new high-rise hotels beginning to spring up. There seemed to be a new one every time we went, until now it is a concrete jungle all squeezed together, with much less available beach area. Part of Ala Moana Park has been replaced by the Ala Moana Shopping Center. The pace of living seems fast. Traffic on the streets is heavy and constant, even though there are now freeways to expedite the flow. Aloha Tower is dwarfed by many high-rise buildings. Fort Street, the old business district, still has a few of the fine old buildings of the Sugar Factors, but it is now just a small walk-through area

In 1962 the Islands were changing very quickly from an agricultural community of sugar plantations to a world-class resort area. Construction on the first of the many hotels on the Ka'anapali Beach on the Island of Maui, the Maui Sheraton, had just begun. To us, this was not a positive change, and I thought that I wanted to see no more of the changes, since it had all been so idyllic in our experience. When Jim and I went to Japan in 1981 we went on a direct flight from Seattle to Tokyo. But some years later after Jim was married, he and Diana lived in Tokyo for a year. Before they returned I joined them in Tokyo and did go by way of Honolulu, stopping to see old friends and trying not to see the changes. We stopped again in Honolulu on our return. Gabriele and Starr and her daughter, Judy, joined us and we took the seven day cruise to the four main Islands, traveling on the "Constitution", the ship that had taken Grace Kelly to Monaco to marry her prince.

Returning to live in the Islands in 1998, after thirty-six years in New Orleans and Alabama, I am very happy to be on the Island of Hawaii, (the "Big Island"). This is the least changed of all the Islands and has the newest land on earth. Kilauea, the active volcano, has been in almost continuous eruption for eighteen years, spilling lava down the side of the mountain into the sea to make acre after acre of new land. Here we see creation actually happening—plants beginning to come through the bare lava, palm trees and flowers, lush areas of rain forest, up to alpine meadows, with bare lava again on the tops of the nearly 14,000 ft. mountains, which are sometimes snow capped. Geologists say that we have thirteen different climates represented. The trade winds, which sometimes blow powerfully up through the valleys, keep one reminded of the nascent energy that is ever present. It is an exciting place to live.

Since very little sugar is produced now, the "Big Five" Sugar Factors, Alexander and Baldwin, Castle & Cooke. C. Brewer and Theo. H. Davies, have lost their importance. HC&S, the largest of the plantations, had 35,000 acres planted in cane at peak production. Now there are only a comparatively few acres. planted in sugar cane

Recently I have seen the movie "Pearl Harbor". It is a love story and not a documentary, and it exhibits the demand for noise and violence in our culture that has been fostered by television. The makers, the Disney Company, spent five million dollars on a gala preview in Honolulu and invited all the remaining veterans of the Japanese attack to come and be a part of it. A stadium holding 2000 people was constructed on the flight deck of a carrier in port, with red carpeting leading to the center stage. The stars of the movie were there, of course, but local news focused on the veterans and some wonderful stories were told.

A new "coffee table" book has been published depicting the history of Waikiki for the past 500 years. A video preview was held at one of the Kohala beach hotels. When the story got to modern times, I began to realize that I had experienced most of the changes. Before the war Waikiki was a quiet, relaxing place for swimming and sunbathing on uncrowded beaches, with a few fun places for evening entertainment. The old Waikiki Theater where I saw the new movie "*Gone With the Wind*" in 1939 had an organ for mood music and intermissions. I went to the Banyan Court at the Moana Hotel when Harry Owens broadcast his Saturday morning "Hawaii Calls" programs. I danced to his music at the Royal Hawaiian Hotel. The movie stars were beginning to come, delighted to be somewhere they were not hounded for autographs. (I remember one night being on the dance floor with Joan Crawford and thinking how beautiful she was in real life.) Kapiʻolani Park had Saturday morning programs of Hawaiian music and hula dancing put on by the Kodak Company.

Those are my happy memories, but Waikiki is a special place, hardly related to the every-day life of most of the population.

Now, Kalakaua Avenue, between King Street and Waikiki is not recognizable, with its small buildings all along the avenue ending in a tangle of high rise office buildings and hotels. The fine small building that housed Gump's import shop is still there, but the Royal Hawaiian Hotel is completely hidden by a shopping mall. The Halekulani Hotel has been entirely rebuilt and is tucked in among other hotels. The grand old Moana Hotel still has dignity, standing just by Kuhio Beach.

The Outdoor Circle continues to be a very important organization in the beautification of the Islands as they change. There are branches of the Outdoor Circle on each of the larger islands, actively monitoring changes, planting trees and improving roadways with trees and shrubbery.

In the past hundred years the Islands have become a true melting pot of nationalities, with intermarriages making all sorts of combinations of races living in peaceful coexistence. Native Hawaiians, however, have felt themselves to be a very much ignored minority in what used to be their sovereign land. The civil rights movement on the Mainland seems to have been the catalyst for a reawakening to all that was being lost. Few owned land, and it appeared that every vestige of their culture was being lost before the onslaught of the bulldozers of "developers". The sacred places had fallen into ruins, burial sites were not honored, the good beaches were being appropriated for tourist hotels, and the Hawaiian language was almost forgotten.

"Immersion" schools in which only Hawaiian is spoken are now on each of the islands. Some of the great *heiau* (temples) have been restored or rebuilt. The ancient stories are being told in books and in songs and hula. The three day "Merrie Monarch Festival" is held each spring in Hilo, on the island of Hawaii, honoring King Kalakaua III, the monarch who restored the performance of the hula. Hula schools (*halau*) from the other islands come and perform in competition, bringing back the ancient stories and costumes. King Kamehameha the Great, who united the islands into one kingdom, is honored on his birthday with parades, and his two seven foot life-size statues are lavishly decorated with leis of all kinds. Some Hawaiians are even asking for the restoration of some of their land, and the establishment of a separate kingdom. Plans for any new development are supposed to be carefully examined, although all efforts at preservation require constant vigilance, and too often the bulldozer seems to precede the environmental impact study.

In the 1970's the idea of repeating the original journey to Hawaii was conceived. A large outrigger canoe was built, using the only the tools and materials available to the ancients. No one could be found to do the tremendous job of making the sails of finely woven lauhala, so the sails were of nylon. One person in all of the Pacific isles was found who had the necessary knowledge of the old methods of navigation to teach a crew of young sailors. The sailing canoe, the Hokule'a, named for the star *Arcturus*, was built, and several successful voyages to Tahiti, the Marquesas and other islands of the Pacific have been completed, using only the stars, the winds and the currents for navigation, thus proving the amazing competency of the ancient Pacific Islanders.

The making of small outrigger canoes has been revived, using the old methods of construction—with appropriate kinds of woods for the various parts and coconut fiber cordage for binding. The art of making *kapa* (non-woven cloth), of fine lauhala weaving for hats, and of featherwork for leis to decorate them is being learned again. Flower leis and leis of seeds and small shells of almost infinite variety are being seen. Chanted Hawaiian *pule* (prayers) are heard at the opening of meetings of dedication and celebration. Many of Hawaii's "Living Treasures" who are reviving these arts and crafts live here on the Island of Hawaii.

On July 8, 2000, Helen Weiss and I had an appointment to visit the beautiful facilities in the very up-to-date Queen's Hospital laboratories. We were shown all of the new rooms where the laboratory procedures are done, by the manager, William Lewis, who came to meet us on his day off. He had some old records to show us in his office, asked us questions, and listened as we reminisced—to our great delight. We were very grateful to Mr. Lewis and to Vice President Karen Muranaka for arranging the interview. The only disappointment was that the hospital's history room was closed on the weekend, and that we did not get to meet with the historian, Margery Hastert. At a later date, Helen and I did visit the historical room when there was an exhibit of early WWII records. Mrs. Hastert thanked me for my account of "The Day the Sky Fell", which I had written for their records, and graciously searched out copies of the Medical Director, Dr. N. P. Larsen's annual hospital reports for the years that we were employed there. We were pleased to find that we were recognized in the historical records.

On October 17, 2000, Jim and his wife Diana and I took a

trip to Maui. We visited Alex and Mary Jane Mc Barnet, who lived across the street from us in Sprecklesville in the 1950's. We took with us a picture which their son, Terry, made when he was a Boy Scout. The picture, made of small pieces of colored beach glass, was of a fish swimming over rocks. The pieces of glass were glued to a backing of foil, which gave the effect of sparkling water. I had enjoyed the picture for all these years, but I wanted to be sure that it was returned to Mary Jane and Terry.

We drove all around Sprecklesville (named for Claus Spreckles, the sugar rival of Mr. H.P. Baldwin, the winner-take-all in the irrigation ditch completion race). Of course we drove past our dream house at 201 Kealakai Place, and I reminisced that a neighbor, Bea Savage, and I had named the streets of the new subdivision by the Country Club. Now there are street signs and many more homes along the beach.

The focus of the trip was to revisit the rain forest area of East Maui where we lived when we first went to Maui in 1945. We knew that a county agency arranged regular meetings of the kupuna (elderly) in each district, and we wanted to attend such a meeting in the hopes of finding some who remembered our time there with the East Maui Irrigation Company. We learned of a man from Ke'anae who had gone to a retirement community in Kahului and gave him a call. He said that he had worked for E.M.I. and remembered "Mr. Thomas. Nice man." This was just what we were hoping for.

On October 18th we took Mr. Jimmy Hueu with us along the Hana Road, now the Hana Highway. Mr. Hueu proved to be a very knowledgeable historian with a wonderful memory of times and places. We were very glad that we had a tape recorder with us. He could name every gulch along the way and pointed out where each of the four main irrigation ditches originated and where they flowed. Mr. Hueu recounted stories of the places we passed. He said that so much of Hawaiian history has been lost or revised that the history is "turned backside down"! His parents did not even speak the Hawaiian language, even though they lived in a remote area where there were many native Hawaiians. He had to learn the Hawaiian language from his grandparents.

The foliage has grown so in the intervening years that we could never possibly have located where our house was in Kailua. Mr. Hueu told us to turn onto a tiny little almost overgrown road that wound up the hill to where the house once stood. The house, the washhouse and the garage are all gone. A rather new house stands in the same spot. When we lived there we could look down the mountain and see Kailua Bay. And the house could be seen from the Hana Road. This is no longer true because lush foliage now obscures everything.

The Hana Highway bears little resemblance to the narrow, dirt road that twisted and turned in and out of the big and little canyons for all those miles. Where there was only grass, the canyon walls are now thickly covered with trees of many varieties and sizes as well as 100 ft. tall bamboo. Now when I see T shirts with the inscription "I survived the Hana Road", I remember how it used to be. Now it is well-paved and marked for two-way traffic. Then it was rutted, bumpy, more winding, and unpaved as well as being subjected to the daily downpours. The only things that are the same are the very narrow bridges that cross the streams in the canyons. The local people and others on the Island who care are trying to keep these bridges from being replaced with wide bridges that could accommodate big tour buses. The narrow bridges slow the ever increasing traffic of tourists in private cars and sometimes make it possible to stop in the very small areas available to look at the waterfalls. Such magnificent scenery requires time to be appreciated. One real improvement, however, is the placing of railings along the very sheer cliff walls where the road winds down into some of the larger canyons. The Hana Road, now the Hana Highway, is a major tourist attraction.

The spectacular peninsulas of Keʻanae and Nahiku, seen from high above, have very little taro growing there now but otherwise are little changed. However, this is very temporary. The county has approved an exclusive subdivision for Nahiku. Fortunately Hana town is little changed since this remote community is trying to keep its unique character. The road beyond, toward Kaupo, is still a very narrow, winding road, though it is now paved.

We stayed overnight in the quietly beautiful Hotel Hana Maui and the next day drove back into the valley. The day was misty and cloudy, as a day in East Maui should be. Going to Wailuku, the county seat at the entrance to Iao Valley, we had two aims. First we visited the Bailey House Museum, now part of the Maui Historical Society. I had a small part in the beginning of the museum, which we named Hale Ho'ike'ike (House to Display or Make Known). One of the treasures there is an old ledger from the Koa House, a general store in Lahaina in the early 1800's.

In 1843 there is a page listing the purchases of Milo Calkin, the American Consul in Lahaina, Maui. The opposing page has purchases of King Kamehameha III. Milo Calkin was Richard's great grandfather, who had arrived on Maui from Tahiti after being shipwrecked on Starbuck Island. He was penniless when he arrived on November 1, 1836, having lost all of his possessions as well as the hope of a share of the profits on the 600 barrels of oil aboard the whaler "Independence". To earn enough money for passage back to New England his first position was that of secular agent and music teacher at Lahainaluna School, located on the hill above Lahaina. As it happened, recurring attacks of asthma made him leave Lahainaluna after only six months.

Mr. Calkin went to Honolulu, where he worked as head clerk of the house of Ladd & Company. Mr. Ladd was described as a Christian merchant from New England and a musician. He and Milo Calkin helped with the singing at Kawaiaha'o Church and with the training of the royal children at the Chiefs' Children's School. Milo Calkin returned to New England in 1842 and brought a bride, who was also a musician, back to Lahaina, where he served as U.S. Consul. The Calkins had a daughter, Kate, born there, and a cradle was listed among the purchases at the Koa House.

The family returned to Maine, and later Milo Calkin went to California during the gold rush. Mrs. Calkin and Kate followed by way of crossing the Isthmus of Panama on horseback. Kate married William Starr, whose family had the flour mill spoken of earlier which became the large sugar mill used by C & H sugar from Hawaii. Kate's daughter, Florence Starr Thomas, Richard's mother, married Joseph Notley Thomas, a California engineer and a graduate of Yale University; Lake Florence in northern California is named for her. Richard was born in San Francisco on June 10, 1910, and grew up in Riverside, California.

The family of Florence Starr Thomas, Richard's mother, had come to California when there were no direct shipping routes from the eastern part of the country. The wheat grown when the great wheat fields of California were one of the world's great granaries was brought to the Starr Flour Mill for grinding. The Starr family made history in milling wheat and exporting both the products and the grain. One of the old mill stones is preserved in Golden Gate Park. At this same time potatoes were being grown on Maui in the Hawaiian Islands to ship to California!

The first record of the Starr family was as early as 1565 in County Kent, England. A surgeon, Dr. Comfort Starr came to New England on the ship *Hercules* to join the Plymouth Colony at Newtown (Cambridge). There is a memorial to him in the King's Chapel Burying Ground in Boston, and a tablet erected in St. Dunstan's Church, Cranbrook, Weald of Kent, England, and dedicated by the Archbishop of Canterbury, which reads:

"In memory of Dr. Comfort Starr, baptized in Cranbrook Church 6 July, 1589, a Warden of St. Mary's, Ashford, Kent, 1631-32. Sailed from Sandwich for New England 1635. One of the first benefactors of Harvard, the first college in America of which his son, Comfort was one of 7 Incorporators, 1650. Died at Boston, New England, 2 Jan. 1659. A Distinguished Surgeon, Eminent for Christian Character."

The ledger in the archives of the Maui museum is available

only by appointment so we did not get to see it. This was a real disappointment. After our return to the "Big Island", I called the curator of the museum to ask about a copy of the pages from the ledger. She said that could be done and sent them to me. I had them framed for Jim for a Christmas present reminiscent of the intertwined history of the Thomas family with Hawaii.

Our other project in the valley was to go up to the Maui Memorial Hospital. It is built on a hill with a long drive from the main highway. When the hospital was built, trees were needed to line the drive. And, as I mentioned before, our garden in Pu'unene had large monkey pod trees with lots of small seedlings underneath. Barefoot six-year old Jim with his little shovel dug fifty of these in the soft dirt near the irrigation ditch that bordered one side of our yard and put them in half-gallon juice cans. The HC&S plantation nursery had monkey pod trees in five-gallon cans. These trees were not needed on the plantation at the time, so they exchanged them for Jim's small trees and the larger ones were planted along the hospital drive. The trees near the hospital where they get water are large and beautiful. Many of the trees on the dry hillside below are missing.

On top of the tallest mountain, Mauna Kea, there are currently eleven big telescopes searching the secrets of the universe. I am here because my son, Jim, works for one of them, the Canada-France-Hawaii Telescope. As with most of the large modern telescopes, no one looks through this telescope. Everything is done by pictures and computers. James N. Thomas, PhD, is a computer scientist, though he had planned and studied to be an astronomer until he discovered computers while in college. Now he is back in his beloved Islands and working in the perfect place. I live in a small condominium in a planned community, Waikoloa Village, situated up 1000 feet from the sea on the western slope of Mauna Kea, where the climate is as nearly perfect as any place in the world. For all these memories, I am very grateful. Aloha!

Printed in the United States
1245700001B/31-36

9 781401 084516